Jim Tolpin's Woodworking Wit & Wisdom

Thirty Years of Lessons from the Trade

POPULAR WOODWORKING BOOKS
CINCINNATI, OHIO
www.popularwoodworking.com

Read This Important Safety Notice

To prevent accidents, keep safety in mind while you work. Use the safety guards installed on power equipment; they are for your protection. When working on power equipment, keep fingers away from saw blades, wear safety goggles to prevent injuries from flying wood chips and sawdust, wear headphones to protect your hearing, and consider installing a dust vacuum to reduce the amount of airborne sawdust in your woodshop. Don't wear loose clothing, such as neckties or shirts with loose sleeves, or jewelry, such as rings, necklaces or bracelets, when working on power equipment. Tie back long hair to prevent it from getting caught in your equipment. People who are sensitive to certain chemicals should check the chemical content of any product before using it. The authors and editors who compiled this book have tried to make the contents as accurate and correct as possible. Plans, illustrations, photographs and text have been carefully checked. All instructions, plans and projects should be carefully read, studied and understood before beginning construction. In some photos, power tool guards have been removed to more clearly show the operation being demonstrated. Always use all safety guards and attachments that come with your power tools. Due to the variability of local conditions, construction materials, skill levels, etc., neither the author nor Popular Woodworking Books assumes any responsibility for any accidents, injuries, damages or other losses incurred resulting from the material presented in this book. Prices listed for supplies and equipment were current at the time of publication and are subject to change. Glass shelving should have all edges polished and must be tempered. Untempered glass shelves may shatter and can cause serious bodily injury. Tempered shelves are very strong and if they break will just crumble, minimizing personal injury.

Metric Conversion Chart

TO CONVERT	TO	MULTIPLY BY
Inches	Centimeters	2.54
Centimeters	Inches	0.4
Feet	Centimeters	30.5
Centimeters	Feet	0.03
Yards	Meters	0.9
Meters	Yards	1.1
Sq. Inches	Sq. Centimeters	6.45
Sq. Centimeters	Sq. Inches	0.16
Sq. Feet	Sq. Meters	0.09
Sq. Meters	Sq. Feet	10.8
Sq. Yards	Sq. Meters	0.8
Sq. Meters	Sq. Yards	1.2
Pounds	Kilograms	0.45
Kilograms	Pounds	2.2
Ounces	Grams	28.4
Grams	Ounces	0.035

Jim Tolpin's Woodworking Wit & Wisdom Copyright © 2004 by Jim Tolpin. Printed and bound in China. All rights reserved. No part of this book may be reproduced in any form or by any electronic or mechanical means, including information storage and retrieval systems, without permission in writing from the publisher, except by a reviewer, who may quote brief passages in a review. Published by Popular Woodworking Books, an imprint of F+W Publications, Inc., 4700 East Galbraith Road, Cincinnati, Ohio, 45236. 800-289-0963. First edition.

Visit our Web site at www.popularwoodworking.com for information on more resources for woodworkers.

Other fine Popular Woodworking Books are available from your local bookstore or direct from the publisher.

08 07 06 05 04   5 4 3 2 1

Library of Congress Cataloging-in-Publication Data

Tolpin, Jim, 1947-
    Jim Tolpin's woodworking wit & wisdom: thirty years of lessons from the trade.
        p. cm.
        Includes index.
        ISBN 1-55870-719-0 (alk. paper)   3204 6939 2/05
        1. Woodwork. I. Title: Woodworking wit & wisdom. II. Title.
    TT180.T64 2004   2004046085
    684'.08–dc22

ACQUISITIONS EDITOR: Jim Stack
EDITED BY: Amy Hattersley and Jennifer Ziegler
DESIGNED BY: Brian Roeth
PRODUCTION COORDINATED BY: Robin Richie
LAYOUT ARTIST: Claudean Wheeler
ILLUSTRATIONS BY: Will McDonnell
COVER PHOTOGRAPHY BY: Craig Wester

I dedicate this book to all my teachers—including those who didn't realize I was their student.

About the Author

Jim Tolpin has operated a finish carpentry and custom cabinetmaking business since 1969. He has written numerous books on the woodworking trade including *Measure Twice, Cut Once, Building Traditional Kitchen Cabinets* and *Table Saw Magic*.

Acknowledgements

The following people had a direct hand in the creation of this book and I am grateful and thankful for their help: I must start with my old friend Francis Natali who is inevitably the first one to have to suffer with me through the initial birth pangs of a new book idea. Carpenter extraordinaire Bruce Cannavaro was amongst the first to read the outline and offered many helpful suggestions, including an important change to the title of the book. Furniture makers and writers Gary Rogowski, Vincent Laurence and Andy Rae read over some of the first drafts and steered me in the right direction and validated the rather offbeat approach I took with this book. I received further encouragement and tips from cabinetmakers and writers Danny Proulx and Mark Duginski and from publisher and woodworker Wyatt Wade of Davis Publications. Artist Will McDonnell not only drew the humorous cartoons in many of the anecdotes, but he somehow managed to capture my voice in pen and ink. I am especially grateful to Jim Stack at F+W Publications for seeing the potential in this book and for bringing it to fruition. Kudos are also due to editor Amy Hattersley and to the rest of the production staff at Popular Woodworking Books. Finally, I must thank my wife, Cathy Parkman, for keeping the home fires burning while I tapped away for hours at a time on the keyboard.

table of contents

*"The highest reward for a man's toil is not
what he gets for it, but what he becomes by it."*

–JOHN RUSKIN

It all started out in the sunroom of my grandfather's house one morning during the summer of my eighth year. Grandpa Sam came inside and asked me to set aside my toys because he needed my help putting together a cabinet for Aunt Mary. We began by going to the lumberyard to pick up the materials. Walking into the yard's cavernous warehouse, I remember thinking that this must be the largest building that had ever been built. Back home, Grandpa had me hold some boards while he sawed them. He rewarded my clamping efforts by letting me screw in the hinges. When Aunt Mary came home, I remember how proud we both were to show her what we had accomplished together. This was, in fact, the first time I really worked with an adult, and it was also the first time I had an inkling that I enjoyed working with my hands.

Indeed, as my middle school years went by I found that the only class I truly enjoyed was woodshop. Between the playground bullying and the classroom boredom it was only here, surrounded by the hum of tools and aroma of freshly cut wood, that I felt there was something for me at school. In shop I relaxed and focused at the same time. It was a class in which I happily followed instructions explicitly and followed through on every detail. I remember how good it felt to see something come into existence from a little pile of boards by way of my own hands — unlike the rest of school, where things were poured into my head with the expectation that they be spouted back out verbatim through my mouth.

At the end of the year I took home several projects, including a little blue birdhouse with stenciled flowers. The shop teacher, probably relieved to have at least one student who was more interested in working wood than wreaking havoc, had given me an A for a final grade about halfway through the year. He told me not to worry about grades and to just enjoy the woodworking. I realize now that this bit of advice was the first, and probably the most profound, lesson that would be offered to me in my career of working wood.

Then I got to high school, and from there I went directly to college. It was as if I had never worked with my hands at all — or hadn't ever heard about not worrying about grades. Unwittingly, I had caved in to the expectations of my parents and to a society that said in no uncertain terms that only academic achievement could offer salvation from a life of blue-collar drudgery. I didn't touch a board or a tool for most of a decade as I worked my way to a college degree in physical science. I did learn how to think critically and to write technical papers. Mostly though, college was where I learned how to successfully take multiple-choice tests. Having mastered this essentially worthless skill, I graduated with honors and without a clue about what I was supposed to do with my expensive education.

In fact, looking past the campus gates at the world awaiting my colleagues and me, I could see only places I didn't really want to live. I dreaded the vision of myself putting on a suit, carrying a briefcase and becoming yet another cog in the corporate wheel, dutifully trudging to his cubicle every day. The only glimmer of a different possibility came to me in a senior-year English literature class while reading the New England transcendentalists. It sure looked like Henry David Thoreau was having a lot more fun building

and living in a little cabin in the woods than I would ever experience inhabiting a cubicle in some climate-controlled piece of "architorture."

Indecisive about grad school and career choices in general — and having been reprieved from the Vietnam War draft in the eleventh hour after scoring a high number in the draft lottery of 1969 — I decided to get transcendental myself. I moved to New Hampshire and fell in with a bunch of similarly confused college grads and would-be woodworkers. We rented a farmer's back 40 acres and helped each other build a menagerie of rough shelters in which we shivered, sweated and sometimes exulted through the New England seasons.

Though I initially taught a physical science class at the University of New Hampshire, it didn't take long for me to realize I didn't really have anything to teach; I was just spouting off the stuff that had been crammed into my head over the last four years of college. I dropped the teaching gig and started taking odd jobs with my back-40 buddies, doing rough carpentry and cabinetmaking out in the community.

I was making a little money; I wasn't working in an office or classroom; but deep down I was experiencing a mixture of guilt and fear. I could feel the noose of that dreaded blue collar I'd been warned about start to cinch around my college-educated neck. Then I met Bud McIntosh.

Bud was one of the last of the old-school wooden-boat builders still working on the East Coast. Inspired and mentored by the renowned Sam Crocker (whose handsome and seaworthy workboats and small yachts were once ubiquitous along the mid-New England coast), Bud had spurned

the academic life ensured by his Dartmouth College degree to build boats in a tar-paper shack set hard along the muddy banks of the Piscataqua River. My first encounter with Bud was probably the most defining moment of my career — if not my life.

Walking alone into his shop one late summer morning of 1969 (on the recommendation of a cabinetmaker friend who insisted I needed to meet this man), I heard strains of song coming from somewhere deep within the bowels of a massive, partially built schooner. As I got closer, I realized it was not a song at all; it was the lilting lyrics of a long prose poem. It was, in fact, Homer's *Iliad* being sung/spoken in ancient Greek! Watching through a gap in the planks, I could see a small, ruggedly built man in his 60s punctuating each verse with the beat of his mallet on the head of a bronze keel bolt.

It was a revelation. Here was a man, a product of an Ivy League education in classical literature, who had obviously found happiness — not to mention a living and the respect of a huge community of people — through working with his hands. In getting to know Bud on this and many more visits in the months that followed, I came to realize that this man represented the kind of person that I wanted to become. Bud had made it not only OK to wear that blue collar around my neck, but to wear it with pride. Within that year, with great joy and anticipation, I dedicated my life to doing for a living what I had long ago done for fun and pride on my grandfather's sun porch: create beautiful, useful things through my hands, heart and mind — and now with a song on *my* lips.

7

talking shop about
shops and tools

I once met a European woodworker who made a decent living making wooden shoes using nothing more than an axe and a stump for a workbench. At the time I was barely making a living building complex, custom cabinets out of a shop bigger than a cow barn and filled with more tools than a Sears showroom. These days, however, I'm working happily at home out of a basement workshop of about 800 square feet, with an additional outside covered area of 10' x 20'. A partially built reproduction gypsy caravan currently sits in that space, waiting for me to finish its interior. For me, for now and for the foreseeable future, I've finally found the perfect work space. In this section I'll talk about some of the things I've learned over the years that may help you think about setting up and getting the most out of your own perfect shop space.

You will get more done in a shop to which you have to commute.

Of course, the commute can be as short as a walk across your yard, or even down the stairs to the basement. The commute I'm referring to is the distance between shop and home that you set in your head — and that you post to other people. The key is to establish a clear distinction that sets your real workshop apart from just another everyday work area for futzing around in. This is the place where you go to do real work: a place where you can focus and accomplish a certain amount of progress in the time you've allotted to being there.

To reinforce this distinction in my own mind as well as that of others, I try to keep everyday stuff like old bikes and dead household appliances from coming here to roost. It also helps to put a "Hazardous Area" sign on the shop door, implying that people shouldn't feel free to walk in without knocking. (A surprise appearance can be dangerous if you are in the middle of running stock through a power tool.) If you want to get really official, you can even put up a sign that lists your work hours. Of course, your family will completely ignore all these signs, but friends and traveling salesmen will get the idea this is a working shop and most will respect your right to work. Even more importantly, you may even start believing those signs yourself!

There *is* such a thing as a shop that's too big.

Having spent the last 30 years observing others and myself at work in more than a dozen different shops, I've learned that a person can take maximum advantage of only a certain amount of room. In large, spread-out shops I'm much less efficient and a lot more tired at the end of the day than when I work in smaller shops. The reason is primarily due to the fact that in the large shop I spend way too much time walking between workstations. Just as kitchens work best when they follow recommended distances between major appliances, so do woodworking shops.

As the typical kitchen is laid out around a limited-size work triangle between its sink, stove and fridge, I arrange the primary appliances of my shop — the table saw, jointer and router/shaper — in a cluster that places them as close to one another as possible. (Of course, a boatbuilder, chairmaker or luthier may have a different cluster of major tools.) In this way, I need take only a single step between where I rip a board to width, joint its edge straight and then rout a shape along that edge (and then perhaps go back and rip it to final width). All those processes accomplished and I haven't walked more than a half-dozen steps! As another example, I arrange my assembly area so that the assembly platform is just a step away from its associates: a counter-height workbench and a clamp rack. This same principle works well for a finishing area and for specialty areas, such as a veneer-press station.

In the years I worked alone, I found that a shop much bigger than a two-car garage was actually counterproductive. I simply didn't need more space around those clusters of tools and workstations. The more space I had, the more cluttered the shop seemed to become and the more I spent to heat and light unnecessary space. Only when I hired a helper did those little shops begin to feel cramped. I could usually, however, solve the crowding problem by simply arranging our workday so that we worked mostly at independent workstations. For example, I would mill out materials for face frames while my partner would put together drawers at the assembly station. These days, my current 800 square-foot shop is all I need. More space would increase neither my efficiency nor my enjoyment — just the area I'd have to clean up at the end of the day!

WORK STATION CLUSTERS

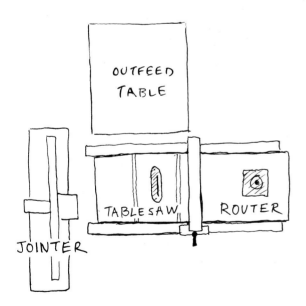

POWER TOOL CLUSTER

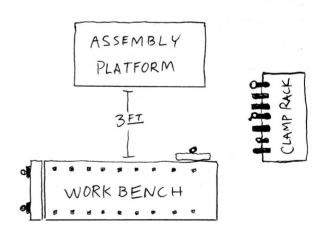

ASSEMBLY AREA CLUSTER

Sometimes the biggest projects require only the smallest of shops.

The size of a shop is not necessarily related to the size of the product made within it. I knew a guitar maker who needed a shop significantly larger than my custom cabinet shop to house specialized stock-bending equipment; he also needed a separate finishing room and a separate, temperature-controlled lumber storage area — not to mention space for all the standard shop tools. I've also worked in a boat shop where the only covered space was the shed that protected the 36" band saw and a rack of hand tools. The boat itself became the shop as it grew outside the shed door. So if a particular product doesn't need to be assembled under cover (because it creates its own cover) or if it can be assembled on-site (as was the case with my custom kitchen cabinetwork), the actual woodworking shop can be surprisingly small, saving you money for stocking up on wood, acquiring better tools or taking vacations on tropical islands.

Work surfaces need to be able to play well with one another.

Getting the most out of a small shop takes more than just having the right tools set in the right places. One of the keys to getting a modest shop space to work really well is to ensure that all its work surfaces enjoy a sweet, synergistic relationship with one another. In my shop, this means that the table saw serves as the benchmark height for every other horizontal surface within an 8' radius of the blade. An outfeed table, a side table (which holds an inverted router and allows me to use my table saw fence as a router table fence) and the top of the jointer fence (a length of wood bolted to its metal fence) surround the saw and are set to that benchmark.

To further encourage synergy, I also built my main assembly bench and a storage cabinet to the same height. Now none of the tables get in the way of one another when I'm working with large components and materials.

In another part of the shop, I built a workbench next to the drill press at the same height as the drill press table to provide additional support when drilling long boards. Similarly, my sliding compound miter saw gets a big helping hand from a pair of tool storage cabinets that I set to either side of the saw, their top surfaces level with the saw table.

The bottom line is that I seldom, if ever, have to move furnishings around (though sometimes I do have to clear them off) in order to work with large pieces of stock. My shop furniture is all one happy family working together to keep me happy.

Some of the most fundamental and essential tools can't be bought.

When I started up in woodworking with my back-40 buddies in the late 1960s, one of the most exciting field trips we made was a two-hour pilgrimage to the original Woodcraft store outside of Boston. On the altarlike displays we drooled at the sight of wood-handled chisels, specialized hand planes, bar (not pipe) clamps and many other esoteric tools we could never see in any local hardware store or nearly any mail-order catalog. (Not exactly the case today if you've checked your mail lately!) Woodcraft was the first place I ever saw a brand-new jointer plane, a cabinetmaker's screwdriver or a timber framer's mortise chisel — and I just had to have at least one of each. Sort of the same thing that happened when we stopped at Dunkin' Donuts on the way home. Over time, I did manage to acquire a wide selection (of tools, not doughnuts — well, actually both).

Then one fateful winter day, I experienced an amazing, though bittersweet, epiphany. I came to understand that tools, like doughnuts, were only a means to an end. You could be a well-rounded woodworker as a result of the doughnuts, but not the tools. This realization happened while I was working on the *Pilgrim* — a trawler yacht I had the pleasure and honor of helping build at Penobscot Boat Works in Rockport, Maine. As I busied myself laying out a curved transom window with my German-made trammel points set to a center point I had painstakingly established with my Starrett try square and marked with my Swedish-made layout knife, I looked up to see Tom Brown — an elderly, downeast boatbuilder who had probably been working on boats since the end of the 19th century — begin to cut a rub rail to length.

To get the new section of rub rail to mate with the section already attached to the hull, Tom had to cut a long scarf at a precise compound angle because the rub rail was curved two ways: to the sheer line and to the outside sweep of the hull. As I watched, Tom simply squinted at the new rub rail and began hand-cutting the scarf with his trusty old panel saw (a shorter version of a carpenter's standard hand crosscut saw). There were no layout lines on the rub rail. Instead, Tom was holding the length of wood in front of the scarf already cut in the rail that was attached to the hull. I was stunned! He was simply cutting that complex joint by eye!

On the first try, he got it "spitting close." He then just pushed the loose rail hard against the one on the hull and then ran the saw through the juncture of the two pieces of wood to make a perfect match. In less than two minutes Tom had made a joint that would have taken me six tools and 60 minutes to make!

Tom had made use of a woodworker's three most essential — and non-purchasable — tools: his eyes, his hands and his experience.

The most important components of power tools are often the ones that you make for them.

There's not much that a power tool can do that you can't do by hand. The thing is, when you add power to a cutter it will cut a lot faster and with less effort from you. That's why we like those power tools so much. Speed doesn't, in itself, of course, ensure more accuracy. That comes from controlling the relationship of the cutting blade (or router bit or sanding belt) to the wood being cut. With hand tools, you are generally moving slowly enough to allow your hand-eye coordination skills to keep the cutter safely and accurately on track. But with the nearly effortless speed of the power tool, things can start to get a little dicey. That's why they put cutting guides on power tools — from rip fences on table saws to base plates on routers. Unfortunately, these guides are often undersized and flimsy and in some cases entirely inappropriate for the job at hand — which is why so much of what you read about in woodworking magazines is about how to make clever fixtures that allow power tools to safely perform otherwise unthinkable (and often truly scary) tasks.

I do a lot of reading (not to mention spying on other woodworkers). As a result, nearly every power tool in my shop has some sort of fixture that I've made to make it safer and/or more versatile. For my circular saw I built a guide that allows me to cut long, straight cuts — up to 8' long for ripping full sheets of plywood. I also built a guide that is little more than a giant wooden framing square. This allows me to use either the circular saw or a router to square the end of a panel or even a full sheet of plywood (because factory edges aren't always reliably square). I've also made numerous other jigs for my router that allow me to form everything from scarf joints to dado joints to shaping along sweeping curves. For the table saw, I've made enough jigs to fill a book — so I wrote one, *Table Saw Magic*.

The key to making these jigs work as advertised is to make them well. I get really finicky about getting tight fits and cutting accurate angles for all the components because anything that's off in the jig will show up in the parts being made with the jig. For most of the flat guide surfaces I use a specialized hardwood plywood (such as ApplePly or Baltic birch) that features greater numbers of layers of thin, void-free lumber than standard plywood. This produces flat, smooth, warp-resistant (though more expensive) material that's ideal for building accurate jigs that you can rely on. I use plenty of glue and screws to join any structural pieces of a jig and use exterior-grade glue and stainless steel if the jig will ever be used outdoors. To slow down moisture absorption (which helps ensure that flat surfaces remain flat) and to keep the fixtures smooth and slick, I apply several coats of polyurethane varnish or shellac.

Until someone tells me what the difference is between a jig and a fixture, jigs will be fixtures in my shop.

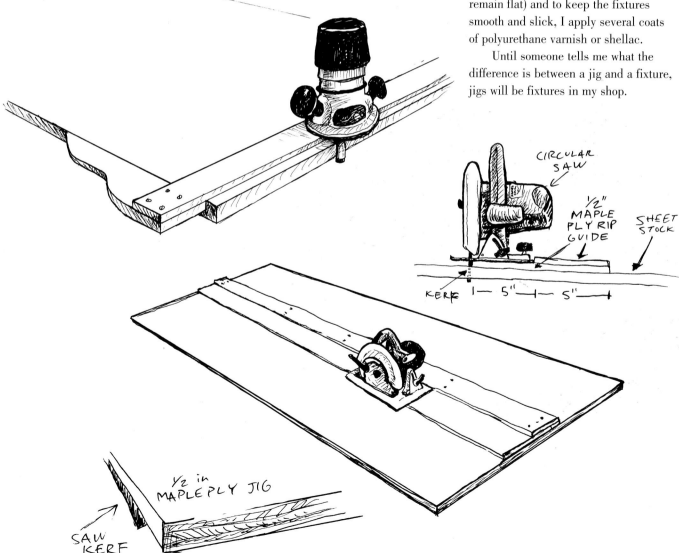

mini lesson

One table saw fitting that is fundamental to precision and safety is not original equipment on most table saws.

One of the most important fittings that I make for the table saw is the most fundamental fitting that should be — but never is — supplied with the saw: a close-fitting throat plate. Most saws come with a metal plate that loosely fits around the blade (so it won't touch the blade through the range of tilt angles). If, however, the throat doesn't fit tight to the cutter, the work isn't being supported in the most critical area: where it's being cut. This means the underside of the cut will usually be torn along the

edge (not good if you're cutting hardwood-veneer plywood and the underside will show). When you cut narrow stock, the workpiece might become entirely unsupported and can catch on the far end of the throat plate and break. The piece usually ends up lost in the sawdust in the bowels of the cabinet, unless it gets thrown back in your face by the spinning blade.

So one of the first things I make for my table saw is a collection of throat plates. Made from melamine to be sta-

ble and to offer a slick surface, each plate goes with a blade. When I cut at angles other than 90°, I simply raise the blade through the bottom of the plate to cut a fresh notch. (After a while I have to replace a plate that has accommodated one too many angles.) In recent years I have installed a commercial, aftermarket throat plate that features a replaceable wood insert around the blade. So, instead of having to make a bunch of complete plates, I just make a collection of inserts.

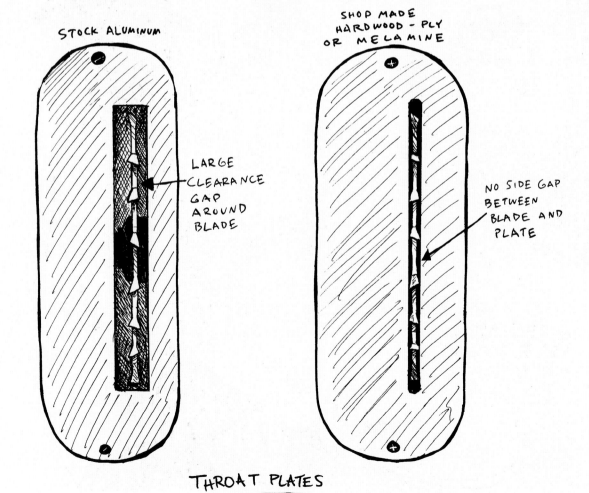

THROAT PLATES

sharper tool talk

Don't work harder, work sharper!

I didn't really start to enjoy woodworking until I finally learned how to get a cutting edge sharp — and I mean really sharp. So sharp that it shaves the hair on my forearm without pulling. So sharp that the blade makes a particular, unique sound as it slices through the wood, a sound that soon goes away as the blade dulls.

The interesting thing is, it took me nearly 15 years to realize that I wasn't getting that true sharpness, 15 years in which I never heard what a truly sharp blade sounds like as it slices effortlessly across the end grain of a cedar board. That's because I didn't understand what I was trying to accomplish during those uncountable hours I spent at the sharpening stones. And that's because I hadn't yet met John Ewald, a woodworker extraordinaire in the Japanese tradition and a master sharpener.

John helped me to understand what a cutting edge really was: nothing more than a wedge of metal in which two planes meets at a certain angle. This wedge is what slices into and separates the fibers of the wood. But if either surface is less than mirror smooth — that is, if it has scratches — the meeting line will be serrated. The bottom of each serration is a tiny flat that will push rather than slice through the wood fibers. The deeper the serrations, the larger the flats and thus the higher the resistance of the tool against our hand as we try to move it through the wood. That's when we say the blade feels dull.

The whole point of sharpening and honing is to make the planes of the wedge as flat and smooth as possible, which in turn makes the critical meeting point of the planes come to as fine a line as possible. Producing flatness takes skill and practice, while smoothness is a function of using the right materials, both in the blade itself and in the tools you use to hone those planes of metal. This brings us to the next secret.

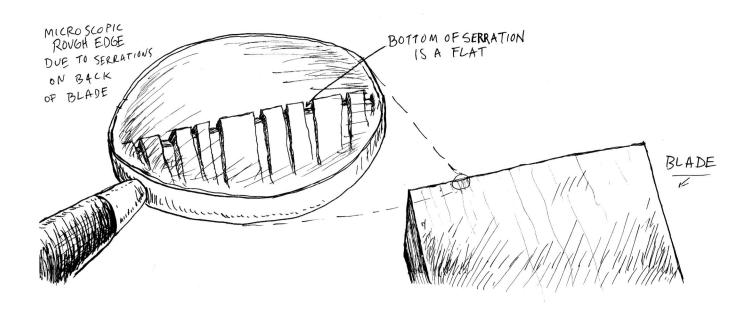

MICROSCOPIC ROUGH EDGE DUE TO SERRATIONS ON BACK OF BLADE

BOTTOM OF SERRATION IS A FLAT

BLADE

A perfectly honed bevel will never produce a razor-sharp edge unless the back of the bevel is also honed to perfection.

Here is the essential secret of sharpening — the key, first thing that you must do if you want a plane iron or chisel blade to sing to you: make the back of the blade absolutely flat and mirror smooth. If the back isn't flat, no amount of work on the bevel side will produce a smooth, straight-edged wedge. When the mirror surface of the back meets the flat mirror surface of the bevel, the line that is formed has only the finest of serrations to compromise the point of the wedge.

I accomplish this feat by first rubbing the back of the blade on a diamond plate (medium grit) followed by a 1200-grit and then a 6000-grit waterstone. (I first flatten the stones true on the diamond plate by rubbing the diamond stone on the face of the waterstones.) I also have had excellent results using Mark Duginske's system of microfinishing papers mounted to a glass honing plate. I usually use a small length of wood across the iron to give me more leverage and pressure. When I'm satisfied with the back, I then hone the bevel side on either my Tormek water wheel or on the waterstones. In either case, I use a jig to hold the blade at the correct (usually 25°) angle. My teacher, John, never uses a jig. Don't ask me how he does it; I just know that he does and he gets away with it.

When the bevel is mirror smooth, and a burr has formed on the back side, I lay the back flat on the 6000-grit stone and rub the burr off. It usually takes only two to three rubs to do that. If all has gone well, I can shave the hair on my arm with the blade creating only the slightest resistance. Another test is to try taking a fine slice of end grain from a soft wood board. If your cutter is truly sharp, it will make a curl of end grain.

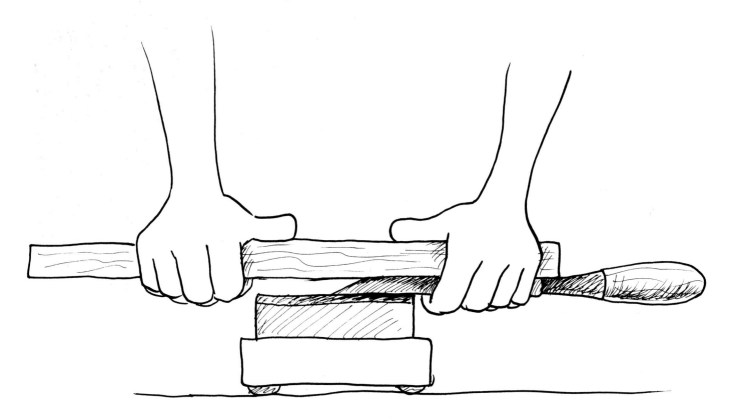

FLATTENING THE BACK OF A CHISEL
THE TOLPIN TECHNIQUE

The best way to sharpen your own power tool cutters is not to.

That is, unless you have the professional-grade equipment, the training and the time to do so. For a while I did hand-sharpen my steel circular saw blades, and I did usually get them to cut much better. When I switched over to carbide-tipped blades, however, I decided my hand-sharpening days (at least for power tool blades) were over.

Here's why: Blades that go on power-driven machines like table saws and circular saws turn very fast, and the bigger the blade, the faster the tips are traveling. At these high speeds, it doesn't take much of a variance in sharpening angle or difference in tip sizes to introduce imbalance and thus vibration. Vibration not only causes inaccurate — or at least wider than necessary — cut lines, but it also translates into heat, and heat breaks down the carbide (which makes it dull faster than it should). There is no way I will ever be accurate enough in my hand-sharpening skills to keep a power tool blade within its design specs. My bottom line: Blades for machines should be sharpened by machines.

Except for this exception: Using a factory-made jig mounted on my Tormek water wheel, I do still hand-sharpen my jointer and planer blades. Because this jig holds the blades securely as you slide the blade sideways across the stone, the accuracy of the bevel is easily maintained. It does take time, but it already takes a good chunk of time to dismount and remount these blades in their cutter heads. The sharpening adds only about 20 to 30 minutes to the whole process.

JIM TOLPIN'S SECRET SAW SHARPENING TECHNIQUE

A power tool blade must be more than sharp to cut sharply.

A power tool won't do what it was designed to do unless it is given a sharp blade to work with, which goes without saying (though I'll say it anyway because I have to keep reminding myself). I have, however, had the experience of installing a fresh blade on my table saw only to find little improvement in the cutting action after just a handful of cuts. What I discovered was that the machine wasn't calling for a new blade; it was crying for a bath!

It turns out that my high-quality carbide blades didn't dull as fast as I thought they did. They probably never had dulled in the past either. Instead, the new blade was soon acting as dull as the old one because the same thing was happening to it: the teeth were becoming coated with resin from the sappy fir that I was ripping. The carbide tips weren't getting dull; the heat-toughened resin buildup was keeping their sharp cutting edges from fully contacting the wood! Using a toothbrush to scrub the teeth with oven cleaner or a specially formulated resin cleaner put the blade right back in business. I shudder to think how much I spent on unnecessary sharpening. Come to think of it, I bet all the sharpening shop did was a little toothbrushing!

A sharp blade is only as sharp as the tool itself.

It turns out there is more to sharpening a tool, whether hand or electric powered, than just cleaning and honing the cutting blade. When I was first learning to use hand planes I focused on getting the iron razor-sharp. Imagine my frustration when I finally achieved a blade I could use to shave my forearm, only to install it in the plane body and have it cut as if I had never bothered to sharpen the blade in the first place. What I didn't know then was how important it was to take the time to clean and to tune up the body of the plane. Resin and rust buildup on the bed of a plane — or the table of a table saw, for that matter — creates a huge amount of friction between the wood and the metal. The resultant heavy feed pressure makes the blade feel dull, even if it isn't. So I now consider cleaning and waxing a tool's infeed and outfeed surfaces (or base plates, in the case of routers and jig saws) to be an essential part of the sharpening process.

The more you sweep your shop, the dirtier it gets.

Once your tools are sharp, you want to enjoy them . . . for a long time. But dust is your enemy. It coats everything in your shop, makes tool handles slippery, clogs bearings and electrical switches and gets into paint, glue and anything else wet (including your eyes). Even worse, dust gets in your lungs. You don't have to be allergic to a particular wood for this to be bad. Cancers can apparently come from long-term exposure to any kind of sawdust. Sweeping makes it worse. You will get rid of the shavings and coarse stuff, but the fine stuff not only gets left behind, but the finest of it (the most dangerous particles as far as our bodies are concerned) gets into the air and floats for up to an hour just waiting for you to breathe it in.

So I reserve sweeping for getting up the biggest shavings in a specific area. After that, I break out the vacuum and start sucking up all the rest throughout the shop. Because I really want to get the finest particles out of the shop, I use a system with a high-efficiency particulate air (HEPA) type filter that captures dust particles down to 0.3 microns before putting the air back into the shop. A standard shop vacuum will get the floor clean, but it will put the finest particles that can eventually kill you back into the shop for you to breathe.

The closer you can get to where the dust is being made, the closer you get to keeping your shop clean and safe.

A good dust mask that really works is great — both for filtering out the fine particles and for being comfortable enough to wear for long periods of time (because dust hangs in the air long after you stop whatever process was creating the dust). For information about my all-time favorite dust mask, refer to the section "My Top Twenty Tools" at the end of this book.

A ceiling-mounted filter that sucks in the shop air and filters it free of dust is also great. Even the most basic units will completely process the air in a small shop up to 10 times within an hour. It's also a good idea to mist the air with water during a heavy dust-making episode to soak the particles so they can't float. But these tools and tricks are just a part of the solution to keep dust levels below the danger point.

The most effective way to cope with dust is to reduce or eliminate it at its source. Of course, the best strategy is to not make dust in the first place! As you will see in another lesson later in this book, I avoid sanding like the plague. I hate sanding to the point where I don't even consider it woodworking anymore. I don't like routing much, either — another big dust producer and another power tool I find myself avoiding more and more as the years go by.

But if you gotta rout or you gotta sand, then it's best to deal with the dust right where it's being made, before it has a chance to get in the air in the first place. The best way to do this is to get suction happening right at the tool. I attach the hose from my Fein vacuum to the bases of all my sanders and to some of my routers. I plug these hand tools into the Fein so the vacuum comes on the same time I trigger the switch. On the table saw, I run a large (4") duct to the base and a 3" duct to the guard over the blade. On my router table, I run the vacuum to a hood over the blade and to the enclosure around the router. Another duct runs to a backboard I installed behind the miter saw. Bringing strong vacuum to the source saves much work for your backup protection systems and makes your shop a cleaner, safer and more pleasant space in which to spend your time.

coming up with a plan

A successful project happens by design — or, for some, by buying a design. The advantage to the latter, especially for novices, is that all the product development and testing is done for you. With a decent set of plans in hand, you know what the project is supposed to look like when its done, and you know — because they tell you — how the piece is going to perform under certain circumstances. You also know ahead of time what it takes to build it because you are literally given a shopping list. Your focus, then, can be on learning and doing the woodworking.

I started out with plans the first time I tried my hand at woodworking on my own. I was in junior high school shop and I wanted to build a birdhouse to give to my mother. The teacher pointed me toward a drawer stuffed to overflowing with rolled plans and templates. I picked out a pretty one and did what the instructions told me to do — which included using the plan itself as a template for cutting out some of the parts. Because I was one of those kids who generally got good marks for following directions, the result was a birdhouse that looked remarkably similar to the one shown in the set of plans.

It took me a while, but when I got confident enough in my woodworking skills to become impatient with following step-by-step plans (my grades in following directions were fast going downhill), I started to develop my own designs. It wasn't easy and many times I wished I could just look up the answers. But striking out on my own forced me to move beyond the fundamentals I had grown accustomed to. It forced me to think clearly in three dimensions and it pushed me to explore a new territory of tools and techniques that I probably would have avoided otherwise. Plus, I got to make something a little different from convention. That, for me, was when woodworking really got fun.

You needn't be an accomplished artist to become an accomplished artisan.

There are woodworkers out there who need only wave their magic wand (or, to be precise, their mechanical pencil) over the drawing board to come up with a perfectly proportioned, uniquely shaped object that works as well as it looks. That's not me, though. I have to work hard to come up with a design that does what I feel it's supposed to do both visually and functionally. It sometimes takes me an enormous amount of time, and lots of crumpled-up paper, to find a solution that does justice to both imperatives. For me, function is easy. What's hard is the pretty part.

It's clear to me (and to many others, I'm sure) that I am not an artist. I am more in the camp of former Minnesota Governor Jesse Ventura, who defined "real" art thusly: "If I can do it, it ain't art." But I can proudly say that I am an artisan — and if I can attain that honorable title, so can anyone willing to take the time to learn certain skills. First and foremost of those skills would have to be the ability to create simple but proportionally accurate perspective drawings. In cultivating this skill, one gains the ability to clearly envision furniture and other projects in three dimensions as concept sketches. This ability can be attained by anyone who can see out his or her eyes, hold a pencil and — most importantly — pay attention. A few extraordinary books can help you learn how to do just that (see "My Top Twenty Books" at the end of this book). If you can find a local artist teaching a drawing course, so much the better.

With practice you will be able to visualize something in your mind and then get it down on paper. From there, it's not a long step to creating full-size renderings or even mockups, then on to working drawings with hardware and cutting lists. At that point you can dive right into doing the woodworking: creating in three dimensions what you created in your mind. All these things — from concept drawings to setting the fence on the table saw — are skills that can be learned by nearly anyone willing to take the time. The bottom line: Don't worry about your credentials or aptitude as an artist; be an artisan. Creative project design is simply learning how to put the "fun" into function.

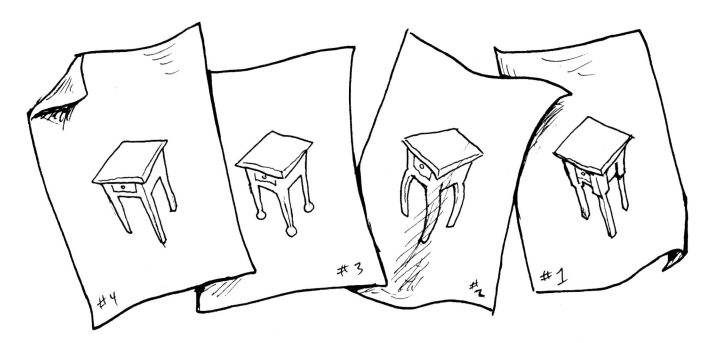

29

Almost any furniture project we can conceive of is a new idea based on an old one.

Now, basing new ideas on old ones is not a bad thing; in fact, it is as it should be. We've been sitting at tables, working at counters and putting things into storage containers for a very long time, which actually makes it easy for contemporary creators of furniture pieces since the fundamentals of design — the way we fit at things and the way we make things to fit us — have been worked out for centuries. So when I start thinking about developing a new furniture design, the first thing I do is look in one of my reference books (again, see "My Top Twenty Books") for information on how to size a particular type of furnishing to fit the category of person I'm building it for. Then I'll go to my other books that show me the broad selection of form, construction and decoration solutions of historical pieces. Invariably, historical solutions are pretty good ones: generally beautifully proportioned and often (though not always) well constructed.

This in no way means I feel bound to reproduce the past — but I would be negligent not to consult it. In fact, I have saved immense amounts of time by admitting that I needn't reinvent the wheel. Knowing past solutions gives me both the clues as well as the freedom to find new solutions to age-old needs. I have discovered that there are indeed new ways to solve a structural problem, and new ways to express the form of that solution.

After all, if I didn't know the past, how would I know what is new — or at least know where to steal a solution?

Ornamental mouldings are not always ornaments; in fact, that is often the least of their functions.

Coming of age as a woodworker in the last half of the 20th century, I was indoctrinated by the ubiquitous style police to think that mouldings applied to furniture were superfluous at best, evil at worst and ugly always. Indeed, I was taught that mouldings were but a curse foisted upon otherwise pure expressions of function-following forms. If I used mouldings on one of my own designs, I would not marry well, my children would be scorned, and my grave would be dug on Pauper's Hill. But after years of building sinlessly simple furniture pieces, I've started using mouldings more and more. Lo and behold, I married a lovely and tolerant woman, my children are far more popular than I ever was around the schoolyard, and I have gotten a great deal on a casket/plot combo from Costco. So maybe mouldings aren't so cursedly bad after all.

In fact, I don't think that mouldings deserved all the bad press they got in the first place. After much studying of 18th- and 19th-century colonial and European furniture, I've come to the conclusion that mouldings were not used primarily for ornamentation in the first place. That's just what we saw and deduced when we looked at them through our Danish-modernized eyeballs. These days, looking with eyes humbled by years spent trying to work out my own designs that would make structural as well as aesthetic sense, I have deduced that traditional mouldings were inherent to the fundamental design and performance of the furniture rather than being there simply to add superfluous decoration.

In memory of
O. G. ASTRAGAL
800 BC - 1920 AD.
OFTEN EXTRAVA-
GANT, SURPRISINGLY
USEFUL,
LIVED LONG IN
SPLENDOR,
DIED OF GINGER-
BREAD POISONING

I've concluded that mouldings were often used to create shadow lines that helped to properly proportion the overall scale of the piece. The complexity of edges and shapes in a moulding were often used to add visual weight to a design or to soften and/or make sense of transitions between components. Perhaps most importantly, mouldings (such as the astragal) were used to hide the changeable gap lines of certain joints and places where components such as doors and frames meet. And that, I'm sure, is just a portion of their past and potential uses. I'm still learning from the past and experimenting in the present.

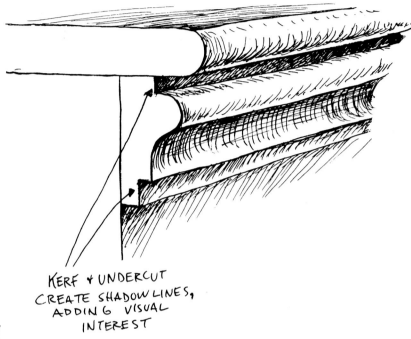

KERF & UNDERCUT CREATE SHADOWLINES, ADDING VISUAL INTEREST

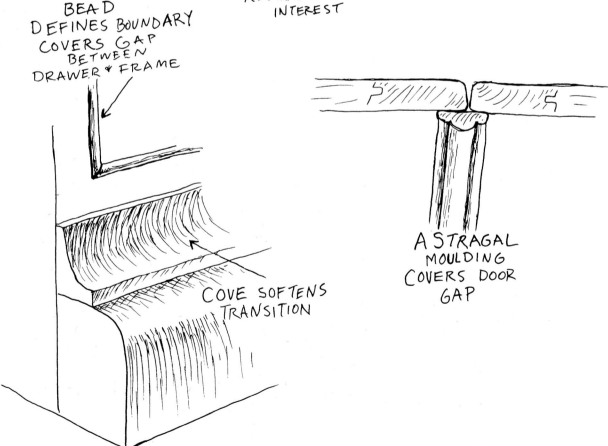

BEAD DEFINES BOUNDARY COVERS GAP BETWEEN DRAWER & FRAME

COVE SOFTENS TRANSITION

ASTRAGAL MOULDING COVERS DOOR GAP

PRACTICAL USES OF MOULDING REVEALED

The best boxes come from thinking outside the box.

So, then, what is my process for coming up with fresh solutions to age-old furnishing needs? What are the steps I take when I hope to come up with the best aesthetic and structural solution to a particular design problem?

I start by posing a series of questions that force me to thoroughly understand the job that this particular piece of furniture or cabinetwork is supposed to do. The questions spawn a brainstorming session in which I'm forced to stare old assumptions in the face and think outside the box. The answers I eventually come up with give me a fighting chance to develop a clever and innovative solution — or at least one good enough to do the job (which means I'll get paid).

Here's my typical storm of questions:

• What are the primary and secondary functions that this object has to perform? (I don't do pure, functionless art, because my mother won't let me.)

• Does the piece need to be versatile so it can have multiple primary uses?

• What are the conditions under which the piece must operate? For example, is durability under large loads a big factor? Is weather resistance important?

• Are there any particular (usually client-driven) style elements crucial to this design?

• Does the piece need to be made from a certain type, color or texture of wood? (Or perhaps made from a specific stash in my wood collection?)

• How did woodworkers of the past address the functions this piece needs to perform?

• What have my contemporaries done with it?

• What works and what doesn't work in those past and present solutions?

After I get some solid answers to these questions I go on to the next step: the brainstorm. I'm hoping to stir up the perfect storm that will give birth to the perfect design solution. The cataclysm is made evident by the onset of numerous penciled sketches, soon followed by a flurry of balled-up wads that fly randomly across the room. I try to let my mind go blank and my sketching hand go free. I suspend worries about getting the scale, proportions or symmetry just right. I try hard not to hold back. I allow myself to get way out there.

I number the sketches so I can later trace the evolution of the piece — a valuable suggestion recently offered to me by Gary Rowgowski, a woodworker/teacher from Portland, Oregon. That way, if I feel I'm going astray (meaning I notice that I've left some necessary criteria behind), I can come back to the point of diversion and begin a new path from there. As the design seems to be coming together, I start getting more careful about scale so I'm sure I'm proportioning all the elements correctly. When I'm real close, I stop and put the design out of sight for a while. I've learned that what I like one day, I sometimes hate the next. But eventually, I like one solution every time I look at it. At that point I let someone else look at it. Not for their approval or disapproval, but for the reasons why they like or dislike it. That forces me to understand and affirm in my own mind why I like it.

Once I have a concept sketch that works, I'm ready for the next step. If it's a small, uncomplicated project, I usually move right into making full, three-dimensional working drawings from which I can then develop the all-important, fail-safe cutting lists (a process that I've talked about at length in several of my other books; see more information about *Measure Twice, Cut Once* and *Building Traditional Kitchen Cabinets* at the end of this book). But if there is any question in my mind about the overall proportions, or the relationship of component pieces to one another or how the piece will work in place, then, for me, scaled drawings are not the way to go. I don't even bother making them.

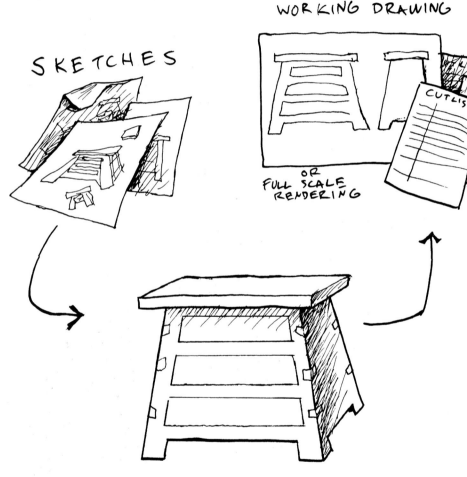

SKETCHES

WORKING DRAWING

CUTLIST 1

OR
FULL SCALE
RENDERING

CARDBOARD
MOCK-UP

FROM CONCEPT SKETCHES TO CUT LISTS

Scaled drawings rarely fully define the full-scale outcome.

I learned the hard way that most clients don't get much out of scaled drawings either. I once got approval for a large entertainment center based on a carefully scaled drawing. When they saw the thing come in their front door and then devour their living room, they almost cried. Of course, I had the law on my side since they initialed the drawing, but that didn't fix our relationship or the monster they had to learn to live with.

So these days I often go right from my concept sketches to building the thing full-size where my customers and I can see it from a real-world point of view. The only thing is, I can't charge them for it yet because it's made out of cardboard.

Once it's sitting where they think it's going to live in their home, my clients can really appreciate the reality of the piece. They can see what it will look like from every practical angle. They will also see how much room it's going to take up; what it's going to be like to have to walk around it every day; how far it sits from where its contents may be used; how it relates to nearby art and furnishings; and how its bulk and shadow will affect natural and artificial lighting. For myself and for my customers, this cardboard mock-up provides proof-in-the-pudding that the piece will work as advertised by the concept sketches. This is essential, because this is the time— before expensive boards are cut (or even purchased) — to make any changes.

To come up with good proportions, all you need to do is look around you; in fact, they *are* you.

One of the most fundamental proportions that exists can be seen everywhere: the whirl of petals within a blossom; the facades of ancient Grecian temples; the overall outline of a Boeing 747; the shape of a credit card. You can also see an example of this proportion right now by looking at one of your hands. Compare the length of your finger from the tip to the first knuckle to the next section of finger between the knuckles. The small length is to the

larger length as the larger is to the sum of both. If you continue looking, the length of your hand is to the length of your arm between your wrist and elbow as the latter is to the sum of both. Finally, the length of your body from your head to your belly button and from there to your feet shows the same relationship. Nature likes to grow things this way. And we seem to be comfortable looking at things that are shaped this way. In scientific terms, this is

called the golden mean.

The golden mean is not the only way to proportion things that work for us visually. We also tend to find pleasure and comfort with a variety of other progressive relationships, all of which can be made sense of mathematically — which is great because that means we don't need to reinvent the wheel for each design. The formula is already out there for establishing the basic, fundamental proportions of any design.

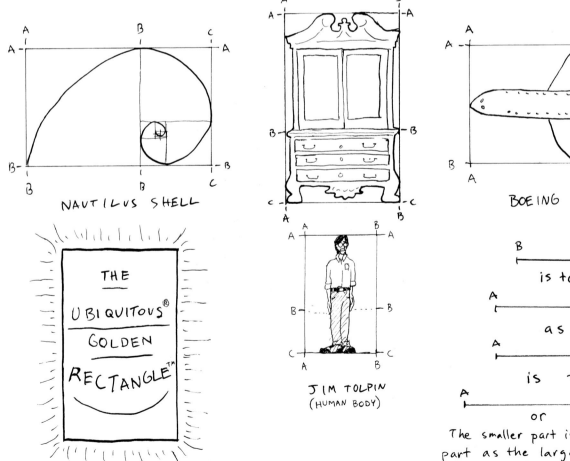

NAUTILUS SHELL

THE UBIQUITOUS® GOLDEN RECTANGLE™

HIGH BOY

JIM TOLPIN
(HUMAN BODY)

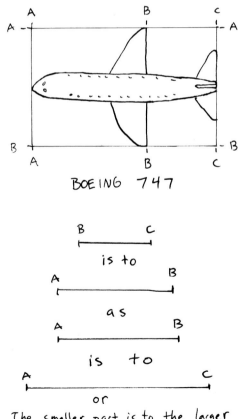

BOEING 747

B   C
is to
A   B

as

A   B
is to
A   C

or

The smaller part is to the larger part as the larger part is to the sum of both...

If it looks right, it probably is right.

Even without the formulas, we seem to have the knack to know inherently when something looks right — or at least when it doesn't look right. As our experience and confidence grow, we learn to trust our eyes and hearts when creating fresh designs, or even when shaping individual components in three dimensions from a two-dimensional template (which is how most woodworkers for uncounted generations before us worked every day). It's a wonderful thing when we come to the place where our eyes inform the heart and the heart informs the head. It is the time when we can take the leap of faith to believe that if it looks right, it probably is right.

IF IT DOESN'T LOOK RIGHT, IT PROBABLY ISN'T

A piece built to correct proportional standards does not necessarily employ standard dimensions in its components.

Because I go so far as to make and confirm the dimensions of a full-scale mock-up of a furniture piece, you'd think I could just plug in the numbers and spit out a cutting list for the component parts. Well, I could if I were willing to standardize the sizes (or scantlings, as structure dimensions are called in boatbuilding and timber framing) of all the typical components of that particular type of furniture or cabinet piece. And a lot of woodworkers do, including myself when I was pumping out production cabinetwork.

The problem is that standardization means uniformity, and uniformity is boring. Standardization must also err on the heavy side to be safe. The bottom line is that a cookie-cutter piece is going to look clunky because a lot of the parts are bigger than they need to be. That's why the typical kitchen cabinet door has one-size-fits-all rails and stiles. That's why posts and beams in timber frames are invariably straight sided. But, in fact, they don't need to be. The top rail of a lower cabinet door can be made narrower than the bottom rail; it will look better because of the angle at which the door is most often seen. All the rails and stiles could be narrower if they are made out of hardwood. They don't have to be sized the same as colonial cabinetwork that was made from pine — a wood that requires larger dimensions than does hardwood for a given strength. Timbers rarely need to be straight sided to offer enough strength to do their jobs; a curve in a beam or a taper in a post are easy to get

away with and look much more graceful.

Of course, these refinements take time, and you have to know what you can get away with. This means you have to understand the characteristics of the particular species of wood you are using and the physical forces that the structure is being asked to bear. But it's worth finding out these things, because the piece will have a much better chance of looking properly proportioned and graceful. And best of all, it will not look like it came out of an Ethan Allen showroom or an Ikea catalog.

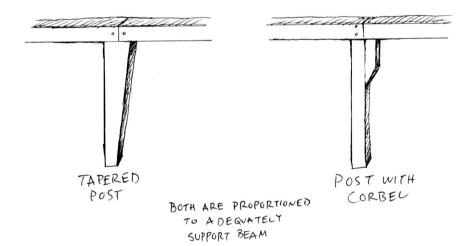

TAPERED POST

POST WITH CORBEL

BOTH ARE PROPORTIONED TO ADEQUATELY SUPPORT BEAM

STANDARD CABINET DOOR

RAILS + STILES ARE EQUAL WIDTH

TOP RAIL IS NARROWER THAN BOTTOM RAILS, STILES NARROWER THAN TOP RAIL

STILES TAPERED

OVERALL PROPORTION IS A GOLDEN RECTANGLE

The selection of joinery, fastenings and hardware can also affect the size of the components and their appearance.

Before I cut any component to size, I've learned to think ahead about what is going to happen to that particular part down the road. Even if I've figured out how big that particular piece of wood must be to support the load it will be asked to carry, other things can affect its dimensions: things like the size of hardware that will be attached or inserted, or the kind of joint that will join it to

another piece of wood. In the past I've finalized the size of a door's rails and stiles only to find out too late that the rail won't accommodate the depth of a specialized mortise lock.

The choice of a joint affects the size of the members to be joined because some joints (like bridles) rely on mating wide bearing surfaces while others (like wedged tenons) may require only one

member to be relatively wide. And another thing: If the joints will show (dovetails are a classic example), they will become a significant aspect of the overall design. The bottom line here is that joinery, fastenings and hardware must be accounted for before you are ready to create cutting lists.

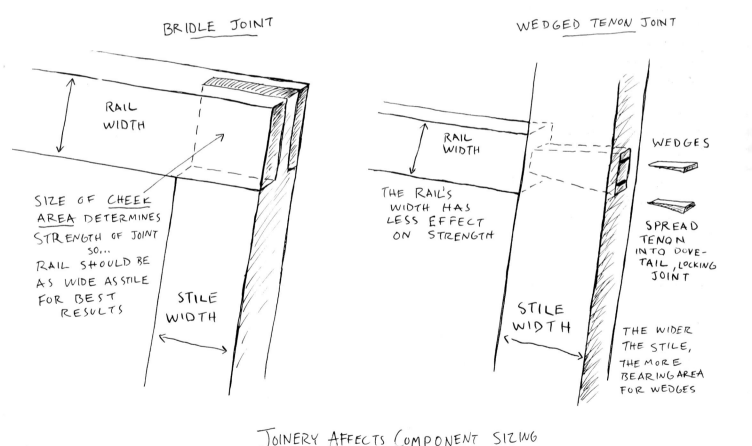

BRIDLE JOINT

RAIL WIDTH

SIZE OF CHEEK AREA DETERMINES STRENGTH OF JOINT SO... RAIL SHOULD BE AS WIDE AS STILE FOR BEST RESULTS

STILE WIDTH

WEDGED TENON JOINT

RAIL WIDTH

THE RAIL'S WIDTH HAS LESS EFFECT ON STRENGTH

WEDGES

SPREAD TENON INTO DOVE-TAIL, LOCKING JOINT

STILE WIDTH

THE WIDER THE STILE, THE MORE BEARING AREA FOR WEDGES

JOINERY AFFECTS COMPONENT SIZING

You will never, ever make wood do what it inherently does not want to do.

Like most kids, when I wanted to build a fort I used a bucketful of nails to attach an army of boards to some random lengths of 2×4s. And like most boards asked to do such a thing, they soon responded by splitting around the nails, falling off and deserting my fort. I never really thought about it until many years later when I found myself pounding nails for a living. While I worked on an old barn reinstalling board and batten siding, the old farmer came out to watch. When he saw me nailing them off in my usual fashion (see the drawing) he asked me what I was trying to do. I knew from the tone of his voice that I was in trouble. Obviously, whatever it was I was trying to do was not what he was wanting me to be trying to do — which was to put on his boards and battens so they would stay there for at least another hundred years before his grandson had to hire another carpenter like myself to come out and put on some new boards. That is, if I was doing it right. Which I wasn't.

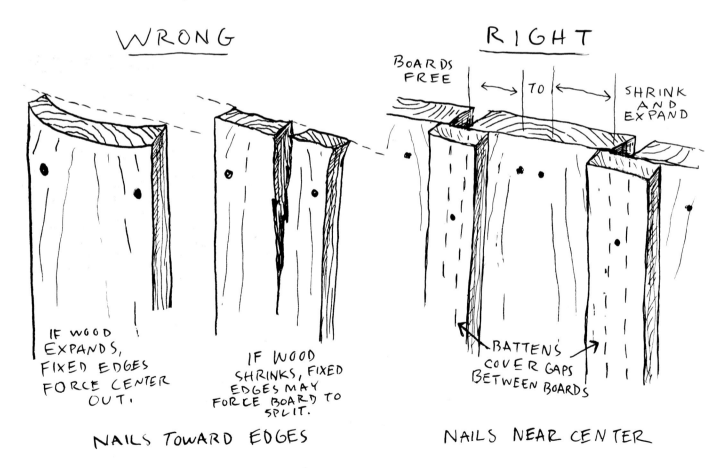

WRONG   RIGHT

BOARDS FREE ←→ TO ←→ SHRINK AND EXPAND

IF WOOD EXPANDS, FIXED EDGES FORCE CENTER OUT.

IF WOOD SHRINKS, FIXED EDGES MAY FORCE BOARD TO SPLIT.

BATTENS COVER GAPS BETWEEN BOARDS

NAILS TOWARD EDGES   NAILS NEAR CENTER

RIGHT AND WRONG WAY TO NAIL A BARN BOARD

What I should have been doing, as the farmer clearly demonstrated to me, was to put one or two nails in the center of the board at each nailing station. The batten should be put on with a single, centered nail, with that nail going between the planks. In that way, the board could shrink or expand with the seasons, riding under the batten without splitting either the batten or the board, yet staying flat against the wall due to the pressure of the batten. What I was doing with the nails was holding the boards and battens at their edges, which doesn't allow them to change size at all. Either shrinkage or expansion would demand something give somewhere. If the nails didn't give, the wood would do so, either splitting down the middle during shrink-age or bowing during expansion.

I learned that day that I should never try to make wood do what it inherently does not want to do, because I won't win. (In the case of the farmer, I wouldn't have gotten paid either.) This basic principle has affected the way I've designed and constructed nearly every woodworking project I've built since. I now understand why the woodworkers of the Middle Ages invented the frame and panel and why later generations invented plywood. I understand why some mouldings are common in furniture and why mortise-and-tenon joints have internal gaps. These are all fundamental strategies to deal effectively with the inherent, changeable nature of wood.

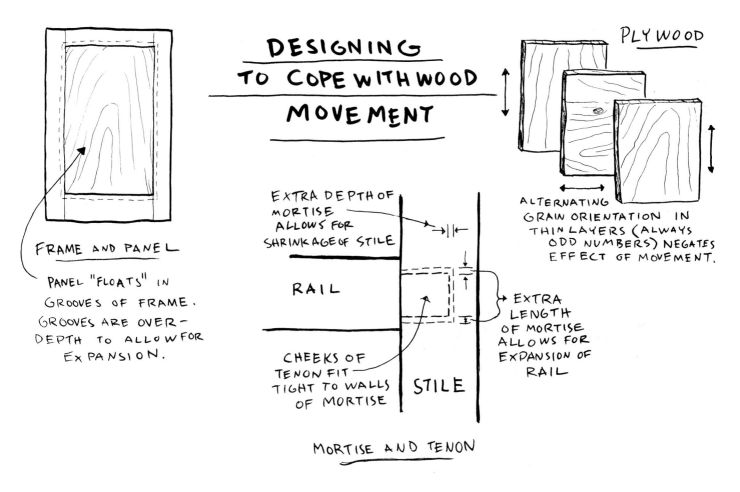

DESIGNING TO COPE WITH WOOD MOVEMENT

FRAME AND PANEL

PANEL "FLOATS" IN GROOVES OF FRAME. GROOVES ARE OVER-DEPTH TO ALLOW FOR EXPANSION.

EXTRA DEPTH OF MORTISE ALLOWS FOR SHRINKAGE OF STILE

RAIL

CHEEKS OF TENON FIT TIGHT TO WALLS OF MORTISE

STILE

EXTRA LENGTH OF MORTISE ALLOWS FOR EXPANSION OF RAIL

MORTISE AND TENON

PLYWOOD

ALTERNATING GRAIN ORIENTATION IN THIN LAYERS (ALWAYS ODD NUMBERS) NEGATES EFFECT OF MOVEMENT.

Plywood is overrated.

If those barn boards had been made out of plywood, I could have nailed the bejeezus out of them and they would have not complained a bit. Plywood has an incredible resistance to shrinkage and expansion since the layers from which plywood are made are extremely thin and lay 90° offset to one another. Cutting boards from the sheets would have been efficient as there would have been literally no waste, as there usually is when sizing raw lumber to width and length. If I wanted lengths more than the standard 8' sheet would provide, I could easily (with a router and jig setup) create a glue scarf to extend the sheet.

But plywood is not always the best or most appropriate alternative to plain old wood. It is a good choice when stability and material efficiency are the highest priority. It is also a way to ensure uniform — though often bland — color and figure throughout a project. This is why plywood (or other sheet goods) is used extensively throughout the cabinetmaking industry. It is also why I try to avoid commercial plywood for the parts of my cabinets and furnishings that show. I like the uniqueness and variability of real wood. I like knowing each board personally and deciding where to use it to take best advantage of its appearance. I love mating boards edge to edge and choosing grain patterns that complement each other.

I also like the fact that real wood is real all the way through. With commercial plywood only a fraction of an inch is the wood you want to show (so you'd better not sand through it, or shape it, texture it or do the things that can make a real wood surface uniquely handcrafted). It's also important to note that except in the highest grade (read *expensive*) plywoods, the interior veneers may be of poor quality with defects and outright voids that significantly weaken the product. But most of all I appreciate the depth of real wood that makes itself known when you apply penetrating-oil-type finishes. I have never seen a plywood veneer exhibit the depth of finish that a solid-wood board can. And one last thing (though not least when you are designing shelving): the cheapest pine board will carry more weight without sagging than the fanciest grade of plywood or other sheet stock.

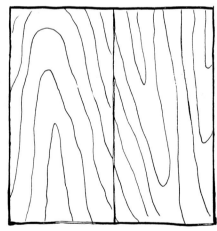

GRAIN FLOWS FROM ONE BOARD TO ANOTHER

BOARDS "BOOK-MATCHED" BY RIPSAWING TO HALF THICKNESS AND JOINING INSIDE EDGES

MELDING GRAIN PATTERNS

TO HIDE OR ENHANCE JOINTS

Sometimes the best plywood you can get is not for sale at the lumberyard.

One of my longtime clients asked me to create a dining table with one simple criterion: the design should incorporate a large sheet of black granite framed with cherry wood. While we talked I sketched. One doodle caught their eye and they went for it full tilt: the granite surrounded by 8"-wide boards miter-joined at the four corners. Great, I thought to myself, now how am I going to pull that off?

The problem with wide miters is that any change in the width of the boards shows up as a gap — either at the inside or outside corner. Another problem with my concept is that granite doesn't move and wood does. If I were to tightly frame the stone with the wood as my sketch implied, and the wood were to expand, there would be hell to pay (and not me if it happened before the final installment). One solution would be to use cherry-faced plywood. The high dimensional stability of plywood would eliminate these problems.

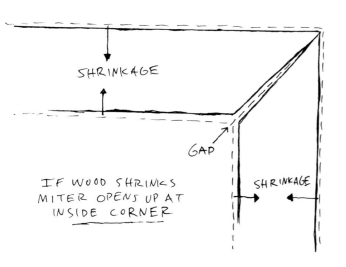

SHRINKAGE

GAP

SHRINKAGE

IF WOOD SHRINKS MITER OPENS UP AT INSIDE CORNER

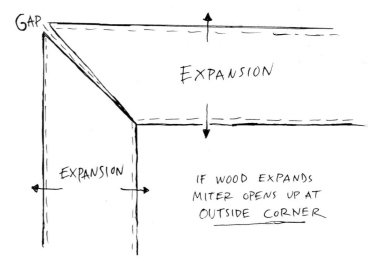

GAP

EXPANSION

EXPANSION

IF WOOD EXPANDS MITER OPENS UP AT OUTSIDE CORNER

But the trouble with that solution was a deal buster: The clients didn't like the bland look of cherry plywood any more than I did. The veneers of even the highest grades of commercial hardwood plywood are very thin; so thin that you can practically see through them. Thin veneers just don't have the depth to create the rich finish that we were looking for. In fact, the other solid-cherry wood furnishings I had built had spoiled them forever. The plywood sample — though similarly finished with hand-rubbed penetrating oils — just didn't come close.

We didn't want to give up the idea of miters, so I decided that if I couldn't buy plywood with a thick-enough veneer, then I could make it. This strategy is not all that innovative or uncommon. The desktops of some Craftsman-era pieces were made by gluing three to five layers of oak strips at right angles to one another. The result was a stable, wide surface that looked and felt like solid wood without inviting potential warpage problems. If those guys could do it, so could I — and I did. Instead of using solid cherry for all the layers, however, I went with a core of high-density fiberboard and applied an under-layer of $1/8$" alder and a top layer of beautifully grained, $3/32$" cherry. Today, seven years later, the miter joints are as tight as the day I made them and the richly finished cherry boards have never picked a fight with the black granite. Maybe I should go into the custom-plywood business.

SHOP - MADE PLYWOOD

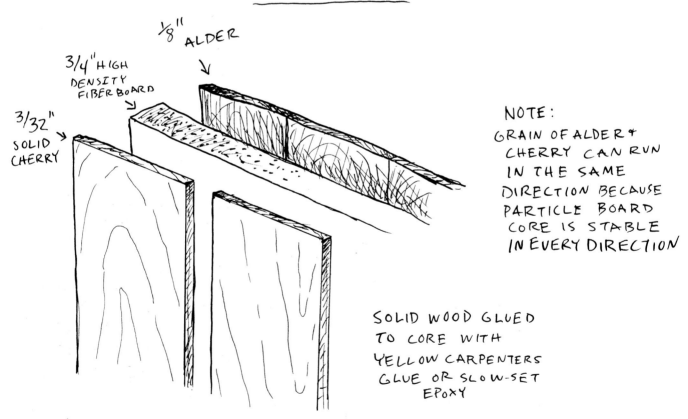

3/4" HIGH DENSITY FIBERBOARD

1/8" ALDER

3/32" SOLID CHERRY

NOTE:
GRAIN OF ALDER & CHERRY CAN RUN IN THE SAME DIRECTION BECAUSE PARTICLE BOARD CORE IS STABLE IN EVERY DIRECTION

SOLID WOOD GLUED TO CORE WITH YELLOW CARPENTERS GLUE OR SLOW-SET EPOXY

Dovetails are not the holy grail of woodworking.

Don't get me wrong; dovetails are beautiful. They are challenging and fun to make, and they do what they were designed to do superbly — which is to provide a full board-width joint at a corner where there will be no shear forces. Because of the abundant meeting surface of all the pins and tails taken together, no fasteners other than glue are needed to keep the joint together. Another benefit for the traditional craftsman is that dovetails are relatively easy (and quick with practice) to cut with basic hand tools. Of course, these days numerous fixtures are available for cutting them with routers or even table saws. And, oh yes, the dovetail is an interesting joint to look at.

Sometimes too interesting, however. Before our generation came along, dovetails were considered more for their functional rather than aesthetic virtues. I've seen many examples of 18th- and 19th-century furniture where finely crafted dovetails were hidden under mouldings or used in out-of-sight areas. In many furniture designs these days, dovetails seem to be on full display — almost as if the cabinet is but a backboard for the gee-whiz appeal of a many-pinned dovetail. You can even buy router fixtures that give you the ability to outline the pins with another wood so they announce themselves even more loudly.

In my designs, however, I like to see the overall form of the object speak louder than its details. No amount of fancy joinery will make up for graceless proportions. I also like to choose joints that are appropriate to the situation, not automatically go with the one with the biggest gee-whiz factor. After all, there is no one right joint. A joint is right if it does what it's supposed to do. A butt joint with a couple of nails to hold it together is not necessarily a bad joint if it is appropriate to the application. Likewise, the finest French dovetail might be absolutely inappropriate, not only because it may be overkill and look totally out of place, but because it may be structurally flawed, as tension works only when resistance is applied perfectly parallel to its pins and tails.

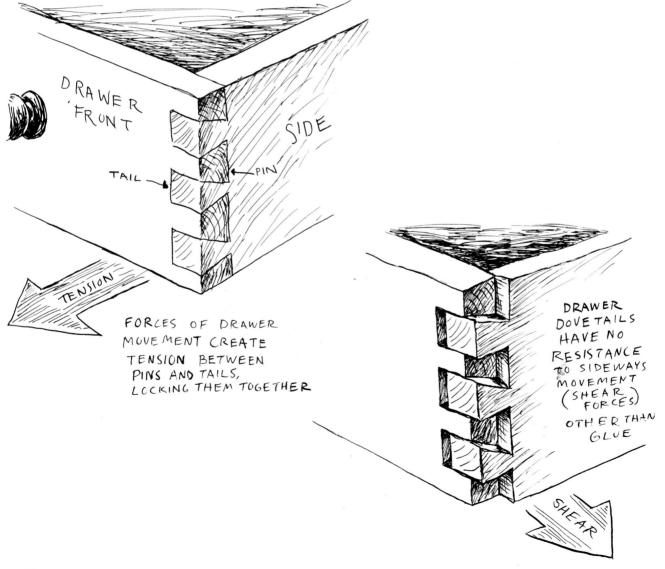

DRAWER FRONT

SIDE

TAIL

PIN

TENSION

FORCES OF DRAWER MOVEMENT CREATE TENSION BETWEEN PINS AND TAILS, LOCKING THEM TOGETHER

DRAWER DOVETAILS HAVE NO RESISTANCE TO SIDEWAYS MOVEMENT (SHEAR FORCES) OTHER THAN GLUE

SHEAR

Dowel joints are foul joints.

"Oh look, dear, this furniture was put together by a real craftsman. You can see where he used real dowels to hold it together!" When I worked the craft fair circuit many years ago, I heard that exclamation a number of times as people looked over my pinned-tenon cabinets. For some reason I have yet to fath-om, if the average consumer saw what looked like a dowel, they believed it to be evidence of true craftsmanship. I kept my mouth shut at the time because although there wasn't a dowel anywhere near my cabinets, the fact that people thought so did result in some sales. If they had asked me, though, here's what I would have said (and did say to a handful of people who seemed interested enough to listen to my spiel).

"No, those aren't dowels holding my cabinets together. Those are hand-made, octagonal-sided ironbark pegs that *help* hold my cabinets together. I don't use store-bought round dowels, because I prefer to use a harder wood of known quality. Also, the octagonal facets ensure the peg won't work loose — unlike a round dowel that can potentially loosen over time as the peg hole seasonally changes shape. I drove the pegs through an offset hole in the tenon, which works to draw the shoulders of the joint tightly together and also serves to physically hold the joint together when (not if) the glue fails someday."

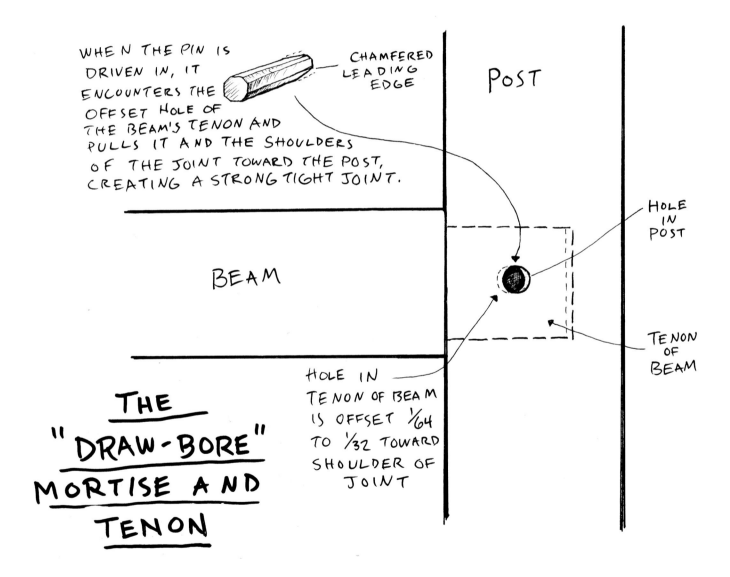

WHEN THE PIN IS DRIVEN IN, IT ENCOUNTERS THE OFFSET HOLE OF THE BEAM'S TENON AND PULLS IT AND THE SHOULDERS OF THE JOINT TOWARD THE POST, CREATING A STRONG TIGHT JOINT.

CHAMFERED LEADING EDGE

POST

HOLE IN POST

BEAM

TENON OF BEAM

HOLE IN TENON OF BEAM IS OFFSET 1/64 TO 1/32 TOWARD SHOULDER OF JOINT

THE "DRAW-BORE" MORTISE AND TENON

If they are still showing interest, I'll explain to them that I never use dowels to hold a cabinet together. I never, for example, use them as a substitute for tenons for at least three reasons. First, a round tenon has only a minimal amount of meeting surface area compared to a flat-sided tenon (see drawing), making it more subject to failure. Second, the round tenon doesn't offer enough surface area for effective pegging or wedging — both important to making a mortise-and-tenon joint independent of glue for strength. And finally, a dowel tenon is a pain to use because of the necessity to make the receiving holes in both members precisely centered and parallel with one another. If they are off at all, the joint will be out of alignment and difficult to fix without weakening the joint (because you have to shave off areas of the tenon). These days, about the only use I have for store-bought dowels is making curtain rods for dollhouses.

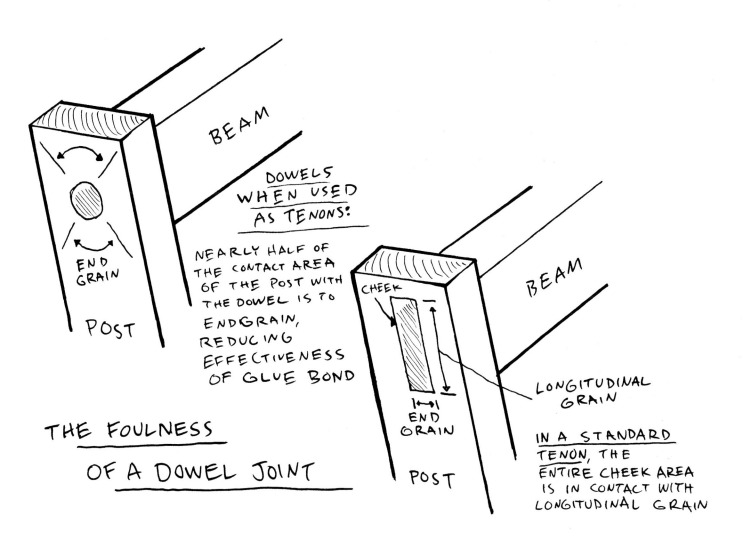

BEAM

DOWELS WHEN USED AS TENONS:

NEARLY HALF OF THE CONTACT AREA OF THE POST WITH THE DOWEL IS TO ENDGRAIN, REDUCING EFFECTIVENESS OF GLUE BOND

END GRAIN

POST

THE FOULNESS OF A DOWEL JOINT

CHEEK

BEAM

END GRAIN

LONGITUDINAL GRAIN

POST

IN A STANDARD TENON, THE ENTIRE CHEEK AREA IS IN CONTACT WITH LONGITUDINAL GRAIN

A glue joint is not a joint.

Last winter I built an 18'-long, high-performance rowing wherry. Because I wanted this sleek, lapstrake pulling boat to go fast, I needed to keep its weight to a minimum. I also wanted the construction to go fast, as I was building this boat in the midst of numerous other projects and family commitments. I managed to put the boat together in less than 100 hours — primarily because I used nontraditional construction techniques to build the hull. Instead of riveting wood strakes together along their lapped seams and to a framework of steam-bent ribs, I made the strakes of mahogany plywood and glued the laps (which were temporarily held together with wire ties). In theory, the combined, massive strength of the glued laps eliminates the need for frames (a significant weight reduction) as well as the need for rivets (a huge labor savings). Glued plywood laps also means this boat doesn't leak, no matter how long it stays out of the water. Unlike my other rowing boat, an old Whitehall of traditional lines and construction, the wood strakes don't need to swell tight to one another to create a watertight seal.

I love the new wherry, but I wonder how long it will love me? The only thing that keeps the boat and me from becoming one with the sea is the glue in those lapped edges. I did use the most high-tech glue commonly available for this purpose — marine-grade epoxy. But 50 years from now, I think I'd rather put my butt in the old Whitehall where I can see the condition, and fix if necessary, every inch of the nonglued, riveted lap joints and frames.

The continued existence of the high-tech wherry's hull relies on the chemical bond I created between some veneers of plywood. It has essentially no structural integrity because there aren't any joints. I say that because to me a true woodworking joint is not dependent on the chemistry of glues for strength. That's why most of my hand joinery features physical interlocks in addition to glued mating surfaces. The glue chemicals that we can buy today may or may not have any functional existence in a century or so. I worry that they can leach out, get brittle from sun exposure, and might weaken from working fatigue over time. Modern glue formulations haven't been around long enough for us to know their long-term characteristics. So, for this old-school woodworker, the seams of my wherry are not joints at all; they are potential fault lines. In a few decades I'm going to start worrying about that.

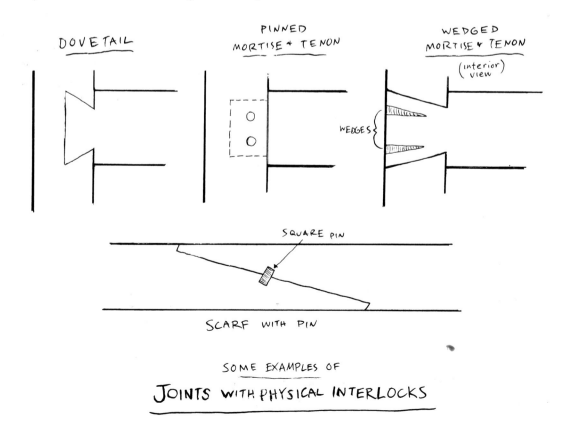

SOME EXAMPLES OF
JOINTS WITH PHYSICAL INTERLOCKS

The faster the fastening, the less securely it makes things fast.

Not only does the selection of joints affect the design of a piece of woodworking, but fastenings are an important factor as well. If, for example, you plan to screw certain components together, you will have to properly size those parts to accept the screws. The head size and spacing of the fasteners can also influence the shape and/or treatment of a component. Bolt heads, for example, may need to be hidden under mouldings unless they are intended to be an aesthetic part of the design — which means you really need to consid-

er fasteners during the design process, not during the construction process. Otherwise, you can find yourself compromising the project by not using the most appropriate fasteners.

So how do you decide just what constitutes an appropriate fastener? I use this rule of thumb: The faster the fastening, the less securely it makes things fast. I've found that the fastener easiest to install, a bright, common nail, has the least holding power amongst the common fasteners that include screws and bolts. A galvanized or resin-coated

nail will hold better (and is slightly harder to drive), but never as well as a screw. That's because a nail offers little resistance to the wood that freely moves up and down the shank (pushing on the head) during times of shrinkage and expansion. All the resistance of the inclined plane of the threads of a screw, however, makes the wood work a lot harder to get the screw to back out. Eventually, though, a screw can loosen, and under a traumatic tension load, may lose its grip on the wood entirely, just as a nail would (though with considerably more resistance). A wooden nail — called a trunnel — is a wood peg in which you can insert a sliver into one or both ends to turn the peg into a wedged tenon. This is an incredibly strong fastener if the peg is made from a dry, sound piece of hardwood. If the member being fastened is of higher moisture content than the peg, subsequent shrinkage around the peg will make it nearly impossible to remove, even without the wedges. But if you really need a fastener to stay on the job through loads that would destroy the wood before destroying the fastener, then you move up to a through bolt.

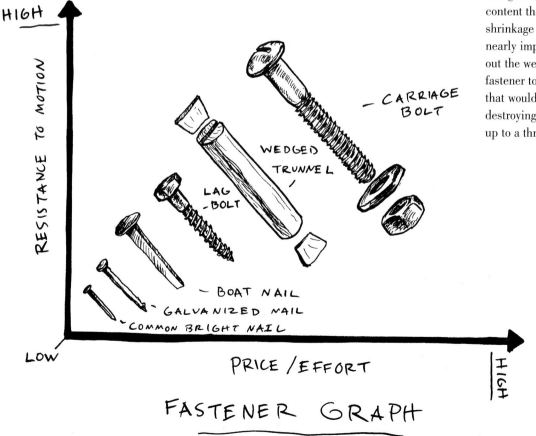

FASTENER GRAPH

Of course, just as in human relationships, the more durable the solution, the more work it takes to make it happen. A nail requires but a few blows with a hammer, especially traditional square nails. That's because a square nail acts like a miniature chisel, cutting its own pilot hole, which reveals a mini-lesson as illustrated in the drawing: The best nails for woodworking aren't round.

A screw usually wants a pilot hole, especially in hard woods. It has to be predrilled if you are countersinking the head so you can hide it under a bung. So you need two tools: a drill and a screwdriver. A bolt is a project to install. You first have to drill the hole, then hammer in the bolt, then wrench on the flat washer, lock washer and nut. If you really want to keep the nut from loosening (which it can if the wood shrinks along the length of the bolt shaft), you may also take the additional time to peen over the threads or drill a hole through the protruding threads and install a pin or wire stop. Look at the wing or fuselage framework of an old wooden biplane if you want to see where someone (for very good, obvious reasons) did go to those efforts.

THE BEST NAILS AREN'T ROUND

A COMMON NAIL'S ROUND SHANK PUSHES WOOD FIBERS APART CREATING POTENTIAL FAULT LINES WHICH MAY APPEAR AS SPLITS IF THEY REACH THE END OF THE BOARD

THE SQUARE SHANK OF A BOAT NAIL ALLOWS IT TO ACT LIKE A CHISEL - CUTTING THROUGH RATHER THAN FORCING APART THE WOOD FIBERS

The best time to begin work on the finish is at the beginning, not the end of the project.

I could let you go on to the next section of the book where we finally get to talk about actually working the wood, but I've learned that it pays to consider finish during the initial design process. That's because the finish usually forms the first impression many people have of the project. As such, it's a style element integral to the success of the overall design. The finish is also the way you protect your project from the overabsorption of dirt and grime, hide uneven coloration amongst the same-species lumber and plywood components and slow down dimensional changes in the wood. So I don't leave the design stage without making a decision about what the ultimate finish will be on the wood surfaces — inside and out.

The choice of finish can also affect the design process in that it may determine the sequence of assembly. In production cabinetwork, I often use prefin-

ished hardwood plywood; the catalyzed lacquer finish is hard enough not to scratch during processing if I take precautions. (I use a wood table insert in the table saw, keep the feed and processing tables clean and carefully handle the panels throughout all the milling

processes.) I also prefinish components that would be difficult and/or time-consuming to finish once assembled; for example, the interiors of drawers. There is one caution to prefinishing, however: You have to be careful to keep the finish off areas that will provide a glue surface.

In some situations, the best finish is no finish at all.

A number of years ago I spent a bit of quiet time in a Zen monastery contemplating my karma. What I did mostly was stare at the board that ran in front of the long line of sitting cushions. This 10"-wide board served as the table upon which we were served our bowls of rice and tofu soup three times a day, just as it had served monks for countless years before me. The amazing thing — and believe me, I had time to notice — was that the board was not only spotless but had a deep, uniform sheen. Of course, it was wiped clean with a damp rag after every meal, but that was, as I later learned, all it got for regular maintenance.

After the eight-day meditation, I asked a monk what kind of finish was on that board; I would love to apply it to the dining tables and other high-use surfaces that I produced in my shop. His reply was typically Zen:

"Sometimes the best finish is no finish at all."

I later got the whole story from John Ewald, a woodworker trained in the Japanese tradition. Because the surface of the plank was hand-planed and never abraded, the surface fibers were absolutely smooth, not rough and broken as are the fibers of a sanded surface (no matter how fine the sanding). He emphasized that an extremely sharp plane blade to minimize tearing and nicking of the surface did the smoothing. The extreme smoothness of the

planed surface not only gives the board a rich sheen, but it also helps to keep liquids from penetrating into the fibers and staining them. It also resists the accumulation of fine particles of grime. Conscientious, careful wiping with a soft, dampened rag is all that is needed to maintain that sheen. If the plank does become stained or scratched, the monastery's carpenter is called in to replane the wood in the damaged area to reveal a fresh, smooth surface.

I regularly use this no-finish finish on my softwood cutting boards with good results. But there is another area of woodworking where I regularly avoid the use of any finish: the deck work of boats. If we are using teak, and the owner doesn't want to maintain a varnish finish, then we let the wood live out its natural life without any finish at all. That's because the high oil content of tropical woods such as teak makes them highly rot resistant on their own. All they ask is to be washed regularly and bleached occasionally to maintain the beautiful silver color created by the normal weathering process.

SOMETIMES THE BEST FINISH IS NO FINISH.

The longest-lasting interior finishes take the least amount of time to apply.

My favorite finish for furniture, after years of experimentation with everything from shellac to catalyzed lacquers, turns out to be essentially the same finish I started out with in the late 1960s. Anytime I went with a finish that sat on top of the wood, I made trouble for myself. They were time-consuming to prep and apply and, being subject to temperature and humidity, often tricky to put on. If any surfaces were scratched during installation and delivery, the fixes were real profit eaters. Plus, most of these film-type finishes really stank during the application process. With the

lacquers especially, you did end up with a nice glossy surface — which some people really like. But I personally never really liked making wood look like plastic. I couldn't see the point of using beautiful solid wood only to bury it under a chemical film that made it look more like a photograph of beautiful wood.

So I've gone back to doing what many generations of furniture makers before me have done: I rub plant-based oil into the wood. I usually use a tung-oil-based product containing driers that harden the oil after it penetrates into the

pores of the wood. The hardened oil — once I've applied several coats to saturate the pores up to the surface — will polish to a satinlike sheen with a quick, vigorous wiping with a soft rag.

If the surface of an oil finish is scratched, the fix is usually just a minute's worth of light sanding and reapplication of oil. The end result is, to me, better than anything I ever achieved with the film finishes. As opposed to a coating, an in-the-wood oil finish draws your eye below the surface, deep into the fibers and folds of grain. It is literally a three-dimensional finish that gets even richer with the patina of time. The film finishes only get rattier as the mouse runs down the hickory clock.

The longest-lasting exterior finishes take the longest amount of time to apply.

In my experience with finishing wood that will live outdoors, I have yet to find any better finish than the traditional spar varnish that boatbuilders and coachwrights have been using for centuries. I have tried the two-part catalyzing varnishes and other single-part synthetic varnishes, and they are indeed faster to put on than the spar because you don't need as many coats. Their manufacturers assure us that they will last much longer than a spar varnish (which they probably would if they are inspected and maintained just as much as a spar finish should be). But that actually is not a good thing, because they are — so far as I've seen — ugly.

When you are looking at clear-finished mahogany that looks like someone spilled a wad of murky plastic on it, or discolored it with a vomit-green tinge, or let a kindergarten class smudge the wood with pumpkin-colored crayons, then you know you are not looking at spar varnish. But if you see a stretch of mahogany or teak with a rich, amber-hued coating that makes the grain of the wood look deep enough to swim in, then you are looking at spar varnish and lots of hours of labor.

Spar varnish takes a lot of time to apply properly. If you are working outside, it must be done at the right time of day and in the right temperature range. It must be applied over a properly prepared surface that involves sanding, vacuuming and rubdowns with alcohol-soaked rags to remove moisture. And that's after you've already applied two to three undercoats of penetrating oil or thinned varnish. Even then, you are just at the beginning.

Because the function of varnish on exterior wood surfaces is to reflect the ultraviolet rays of sunlight away from the wood so the lignin doesn't break down (which breaks down the grasp of the wood on the finish), you need to make that varnish, with its UV filters, as thick as possible. One thick coat won't do it, because it won't dry properly. What you need are at least five to six thin coats with a light buff sanding in between. Some yachts have as much as 12 layers of varnish on horizontal surfaces that stay in the sun much of the day.

Done properly, a spar varnish finish will last indefinitely. Lewis Nasmyth of Seattle put varnish on the hatch covers and rails of his pocket cruiser powerboat in the mid-1950s and the wood still looks as beautiful today as it did the day it got its first finish coat. Of course, Lewis maintains the varnish by constantly inspecting it for cracks and scratches and by removing the top coat every six months or so and laying down a new one. So in reality, the application of the Bristol-quality spar varnish finish is never done. But then, neither are its qualities of beauty and protection and the joy it brings to those fortunate enough to behold it.

There are no mistakes in woodworking, only opportunities to reevaluate the design.

You can, of course, make mistakes doing the woodworking. I know because I've made plenty of them. I've cut parts to the wrong length (usually too short, of course); I've cut the wrong number of parts (too few, of course); I've cut parts from the wrong stock; I've run my hand plane against the grain and made horrible tear-outs; I've . . . well, you get the idea.

Fortunately for me, however, woodworking is an incredibly forgiving trade.

It's not like cutting diamonds or blowing glass, where one mistake is one mistake too many. I can't think of one time when I wasn't able to reconcile my mistake in some way. (I've filled a chapter in my book *Measure Twice, Cut Once* with methods for dealing with miscuts and other mistakes.) I could always cut a replacement component if worse came to worst, though most times I found I could fudge the part to look perfectly OK — or change the other parts to

match. It really helps that most cabinets and furniture pieces are nothing more than a composition of parts. It also is a big help that I treat the entire process, from the first concept sketches to final assembly, as a work in progress.

Sometimes it doesn't even take a mistake for me to change a design midstream if I feel it just isn't looking right. The bottom line is that I let my sense of proportion and grace rule. If it doesn't look right, then it isn't right and I'll do something to change it.

3

working
the wood

I'll admit it right up front. When I first got interested in woodworking, I think the thing that excited me most was the tools, especially the incredible variety and beauty of the old Stanley Bedrock and the English Norris hand planes. This inexplicable attraction was perhaps similar to the feeling that many people have for guns. I, too, remember relishing the beautiful contrast of checkered walnut with blue-nickel metal. I got to see the high craft of gunsmithing in action during the three college summers I spent working at Smith & Wesson in Springfield, Massachusetts. (This was one of the few major gun makers where individual gunsmiths were still responsible for the final assembly of each gun.) But as I grew into my profession, I found that shooting a plane along the edge of a board was a heck of a lot more interesting than shooting a bullet out the barrel of a gun.

Almost too interesting. What happened was that I really got into tools — that is, into acquiring them, figuring out what to do with them and making excuses to use them. I'm still not entirely over it. I enjoy playing with all the latest gizmos and gadgets that my fellow woodworkers and toolsmiths continue to dream up. But what I was forgetting in my novice years was that the tools are — and I hate even now to make myself say this out loud — only a means to an end. For a master wood artisan, that end is to work a collection of boards and/or chunks of wood into something useful and beautiful. To do that well — which means to make something that is at once highly appealing, functional and durable — one needs to fully understand the raw materials. This brings us to the very first lesson of working wood.

To master woodworking, one must master the wood before working it.

I am not saying, of course, that it isn't important to become proficient at using the tools of the trade. It's not easy, or perhaps even possible, to create a truly successful piece of woodworking until one has attained a certain level of skill with tools. But that skill won't fully culminate without a firm knowledge of the material being worked by those tools.

Trade mastery begins with understanding the essential qualities of wood so you can learn to cope effectively with those qualities during the design and shaping processes. Starting with the design phase, the most fundamental and essential thing to know about wood is that it is not static. This is a material that is going to change its shape to some extent, depending primarily on species, orientation of grain and environmental conditions. This sometimes enormously challenging attribute must be accounted for in the structural arrangement of the piece. Furthermore, knowing species-specific qualities such as bendability, weight-to-strength ratios and resistance to splitting helps the designer choose what woods to use for particular applications. (That's why, for example, a Windsor chair is traditionally made of so many species of wood.)

When it comes to tooling the wood, it is essential to become intimate with other wood qualities such as grain direction, density and friability. These things affect how one sets up the tools (for example, adjustment of blade and cutting angles, throat spacing and so forth), how you move the tool in relation to the wood and with how much pressure. As your understanding of wood becomes second nature, so does the skill with which you apply the techniques that give the smoothest, easiest cuts. With time you can even hear, as well as feel and see, when the wood is being cut with optimum efficiency and precision. It's a joyful sound.

THE WOOD IN A WINDSOR

OAK OR ASH BOWBACK
STRONG, STRAIGHT-GRAINED
AND STEAM BENDS EASILY
AND GRACEFULLY

MAPLE SPINDLES & RUNGS
EASILY TURNED, HOLDS
CRISP DETAILING

POPLAR OR PINE SEAT
SOFT... EASY TO CARVE
AND TO SIT UPON.
CUT THICK TO ALLOW
SCULPTING AND OFFER
DEEP MORTISES

HICKORY LEGS
FOR STRENGTH
AND DURABILITY

NOTE: WINDSORS ARE TRADITIONALLY
FULLY PAINTED TO HIDE
DIFFERING APPEARANCES OF
VARIED WOOD SPECIES.

The more power you apply to the process, the further you get away from the wood.

Standing one day at the table saw, about to push yet another piece of oak through its whirling blade to create another length of kitchen cabinet face frame, I suddenly felt apologetic to the wood. I had just realized that I didn't care what direction its grain was running. I hadn't bothered to look to see what the ratio of summer wood to winter wood was in the rings. And I didn't know or care if one end of the board was denser than the other. I didn't need to know these things because the table saw didn't need to know them to do its job.

In my early days of woodworking when I was learning to make primitive (but incredibly delicate and elegant) chairs from pieces of green (i.e. just-cut) oak, I needed to know these things. When I used primitive hand tools to get out the component pieces and to shape them efficiently, these characteristics took on the utmost importance. Standing at that table saw, I realized that I

missed having to know these things. I missed having intimate knowledge of each piece of wood that I was using to create something.

But that was a choice I had made when I moved on from green woodworking to what I hoped would be more lucrative custom cabinetmaking. I didn't realize at the time, however, that what I was really doing was making a choice about how I would relate to my primary raw material. It wasn't until that moment at the table saw that I could see that *the quality of that relationship was inversely proportional to the amount of power I employed to work the wood.*

With hand tools, one literally must stand close to the wood. To use the tool with the most control and efficiency, you have to be sensitive to the grain of the wood, to the presence of defects, to density changes and to many other subtle factors that both demand and reward the senses. That requires intimacy. It is

hard to describe that sweet experience in woodworking when you can feel, see and even hear when a hand tool is working just right.

But as you add power by electrifying the hand tool, you won't (and wouldn't want to) stand as close. Because the tool is cutting faster, there is very little feeling of resistance from the wood and you basically need to keep behind and out of the tool's way. Then, of course, there is all that dust and noise to avoid, which means using earplugs, dust masks and eye shields. As you ratchet the power up further to where you are using powerful stationary power tools to shape the wood, you move even further away because you have little part (or none if power feeders are on board) in directing the cutting action. The machine is doing that for you because now the wood is moved through the tool instead of the reverse.

So where do you want to stand? That is really the question we're asking ourselves when we think about what level of power to use to accomplish a certain task.

Safety is about where you keep your head, not just your hands.

When I first set up my cabinet shop after moving to the West Coast in the late 1970s, my main competition was an elderly gentleman who had worked for decades out of a ramshackle shop hard on the waterfront. For years he had been the only shop-based cabinetmaker in the area, and nearly every Victorian-era house in town had some example of his work. I say competition as a joke, because he was actually rather glad to see me come as he was on the verge of retiring. He didn't want to see his long-time clientele have to go without a handy cabinet guy. Another reason for his retirement was that he was running out of appendages.

In the last decade of the old cabinetmaker's career, the years in which I knew him, it seemed that every time I went over to visit him (my ramshackle waterfront shop was just down the beach from his) he was missing yet another appendage. Sacrifices to the goddess of carpentry, he joked. More like sacrifices to his ancient, decidedly pre-OSHA, industrial-strength machines, as he usually finally admitted. One time he even had a bandage on his ear — but I didn't dare ask to what god or machine that particular piece of his anatomy was sacrificed.

The interesting thing was, prior to this decade he had worked with these machines for more than 30 years without a scratch. It was not the machines that had changed; they were just as dangerous as the day they were hauled into the shop with their cutting blades and belts blissfully exposed on practically every surface. What had changed was this old cabinetmaker's mind-set, or rather, his ability to keep a mind-set that could protect him. That's because without a mind that can really care and pay constant attention to where one's hands are, there can be no safe place for them.

When I operate any kind of tool, from a dovetail saw to the truly scary powered sliding miter saw, I am always aware of where every one of my fingers is in relation to where the blade of the tool is (or is going to be). I have learned through close calls that if I'm using my hands as stock feeders, I have to know exactly where the blade will be exiting the wood as well as knowing where my hands are in relation to the blade if the wood is suddenly ejected from the machine for any reason. If I don't or can't know these things for some reason, I should (and I make myself) use push sticks or other devices. The bottom line is that I am scared to death to use my hands around tools, and I'm determined to keep it that way.

The difference between cabinetmaking and furniture making is the difference between fastening and joining.

In the course of my very first cabinet job I learned one of the most valuable lessons for succeeding at making a living as a cabinetmaker: namely, that there is a distinct difference between cabinetmaking and furniture making. It is a distinction that reflects the inherent difference in the way these products are designed and constructed — which is in turn a reflection of the inherent difference in the way these products will live in the real world.

In other words (specifically in the words used by the boss overseeing my work): "What — do ya think we're making pianos here?" This was his response to my question about what kind of joint I should use to connect the carcass panels of a bathroom vanity. In further response to my question, my boss pulled out a box of confirmat fasteners and a stepped drill bit. This is how I would be attaching the sides to the floors. He also showed me the jig and fasteners I would be using to make the pocket holes that would hold the face frames together. He did not show me joinery, because there would be no joints on this project except in the doors and drawers (which he would be making because he was the boss and got to do the fun stuff). In my boss's world, case joints were for furniture, not for cabinets.

The lack of case joinery was not due to frugality; it was due to the essential nature of the cabinet: a case is secured to, and thus is part of, the structure of a building. (Note: This is also the cabinet's legal definition in lien laws. Legally distinct from furniture, cabinets cannot be repossessed by an unhappy, unpaid cabinetmaker, because they are a part of the building.) The key difference is the static nature of the cabinet. Unlike a piece of furniture that can, and must, stand alone, the cabinet's casework can derive much of its dimensional stability from its attachment to fixed structures such as walls, floors and ceilings. Because this piece isn't going anywhere (unless the whole building is going with it), you rarely need to create wood-to-wood joints to achieve sufficient strength in the carcass or its facings. The only stresses the case is subjected to are static compression and tension forces. Furniture (and, of course, pianos) has to withstand all manner of dynamic forces — including the potentially destructive racking forces produced when a piece is moved from place to place or is played on by Elton John.

STRESSES ON CABINETS VS. FURNITURE

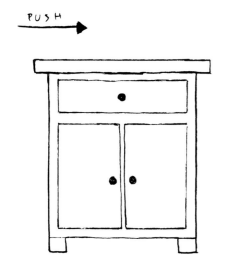

PUSH →

FREE STANDING FURNITURE IS OFTEN VULNERABLE TO FORCES PUSHING AGAINST SIDES

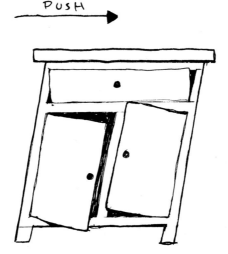

PUSH →

UNLESS PIECE IS ADEQUATELY DESIGNED AND CONSTRUCTED, SIDEWAYS FORCE WILL CAUSE RACKING OF FACE, OPENING GAPS AROUND DOOR & DRAWER FACES

PUSH →

SIDEWAYS FORCE DOESN'T AFFECT CABINET BECAUSE BACK SIDE IS FASTENED TO WALL

The difference between cabinetmaking and furniture making is also the difference between product and process.

Building a one-off piece of solid-wood furniture enjoys a different approach than putting together a box made almost entirely of sheet stocks. The furniture requires a lot more handwork, of course, but also a different mind-set. With sheet-good casework, it's all about production efficiency. My first book, *Working at Woodworking*, is largely about how to make a living building custom case goods in a small shop setting. An essential key to maximize efficiency is to minimize overlap of processes. In other words, when you set up the table saw for ripping, you will rip — as much as possible — each and every last component in the project that requires ripping. It doesn't matter if the parts are in sequence, or have any relation to one another; that will come later. You have to create only one particular machine setup over the span of the project. This grouping strategy becomes a mind-set in production cabinetmaking. You find yourself always looking for ways to group processes. In fact, it's all about the process until suddenly your product almost magically falls together in the last assembly steps before it goes out the door for installation.

Building a piece of one-off furniture is another game entirely, however, especially if there isn't the deadline pressure so common to residential and commercial cabinetmaking. You don't have to think process as much as you think product, right from the choosing of the first board. In fact, the whole project may revolve around a particular piece of wood. Furniture making primarily involves a step-by-step approach, not a cabinetmaker's typical grouping of processes that follow a flowchart. You can focus on individual parts, cutting and shaping legs, for example, before

moving on to the table surface construction.

For example: in production cabinet-making, the process prescribes ripping and jointing the legs along with the aprons, table boards, even the sides of the one silverware drawer. This might be more efficient, but why bother if you don't have to? In furniture making, it's a lot more fun to focus on just those legs first and to do a good, thorough job of it. The step-by-step approach allows and encourages you to carefully select what boards will make up the legs, taking coloration, grain orientation and other factors into consideration. That's because, unlike production casework, furniture making from start to finish is first about the product, not the process.

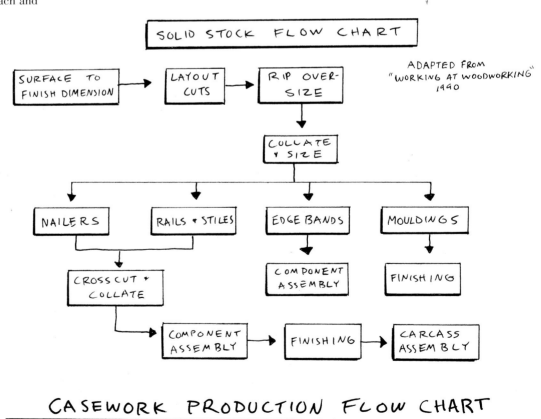

CASEWORK PRODUCTION FLOW CHART

The largest construction can be corrupted by even the smallest component of it.

One of my very first paying projects was a cabinet job for a private school. They asked me to design and build a set of rolling bookcases that would close up against one another to form a fully enclosed box. Sounded easy enough, and I jumped right into the design and construction. Not only was it going to be a fun project, but the easy profit would allow me to buy a badly needed new jigsaw and maybe even a real drill — a Milwaukee $\frac{3}{8}$" reversible! By the time this job was done, I seriously considered never picking up another tool, not only because of my frustration level, but because I thought I might have to sell off all my tools to pay for the expensive European birch plywood I had bought to rebuild those horrible boxes.

Even today, with three decades of cabinetmaking under my belt, a project that called for two fairly large plywood boxes to join perfectly face-to-face would give me pause. To begin with, I would have to make all the cuts for both boxes absolutely square and precise in length. Because the clients specifically requested that all the joints be dadoed or rabbeted, this also meant I would have to cut grooves across the wide plywood shelves with precision (and with no tear-out) and be sure to seat the mating parts perfectly in those grooves during assembly. Even then, there would be no guarantee that the faces of the cabinets would meet perfectly around their entire perimeters. That's because even if you get all the cuts and assembly right, that is not enough to ensure that the face of the box will be perfectly flat unless every part of that piece of casework is also flat to begin with.

Normally, flatness across the face wouldn't matter all that much on a bookcase. Since a bookcase is almost always viewed face on, people are rarely in the position of viewing it across the face where any twist might be evident. Unfortunately, in the case of two bookcases that have to close up against each other face-to-face, the absence of perfect flatness is all too evident. I will say this for myself: I did get one case flat. The other case, even though I assembled it with the same precautions (i.e., clamped to a flat table), came out with a slight twist — about $\frac{3}{16}$" over its 4' width. This meant, as my clients pointed out to me, a nearly $\frac{1}{4}$" gap with the cases closed up — more than the latches would easily overcome with the books and other materials in place.

Looking back from this vantage point years later, I know exactly what went wrong and I remember that I suspected trouble at the time but chose not to do anything about it. What happened was that I made a bad choice of material. One of the full sheets of plywood had a slight twist in it, and I did reject a number of components cut out of it because they also showed the warp. But I remember that I did accept at least two shelves, thinking that the twist wasn't that bad in them and that the case itself would overpower them. (I also didn't want to have to buy another sheet of this expensive plywood.) Well, I was wrong — wrong not to buy and use another, flatter piece of plywood. Wrong enough to have to rebuild one of the cases at my own expense. But I did learn the hard way that just like in politics and barrels of apples, corruption of the one can lead to the corruption of the whole.

ROLLING BOOKCASE PROJECT

HINGED

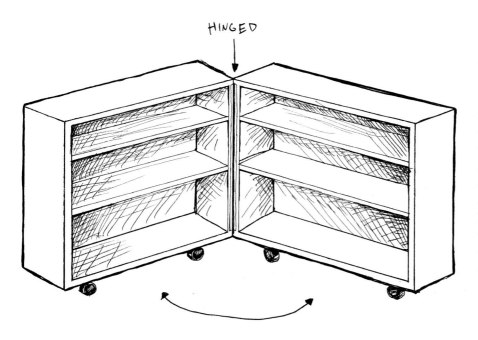

Tape measures don't rule.

It's true and I can prove it. But first — and trust me, you will see why the following little tale has something to do with this book and this lesson in particular — let me tell you a dirty little secret: The space shuttle's design was based on the width of two horse's asses.

Let me be clear, the shuttle was not built to some constant that happens to equal two times a horse's behind. It was designed around the actual span of a pair of horse butts. According to a story in the January 2000 issue of the *Buggy Builders Bulletin*, here's how this came to pass.

The space shuttle was designed to be blasted into space by two huge booster rockets called SRBs. These massive units are made by the company Thiokol in its Utah manufacturing plant. The only possible way to deliver an SRB to the launch center in Florida is by rail. The width of the load that a railroad flatbed car can carry is based on — and limited by — the width of the car's wheelbase, which meant an SRB could not exceed that load width, and they needed every inch of it. The flat car's wheelbase is set by the standard railroad gauge of the United States, which happens to be 4' 8½". That particular number wasn't drawn out of a hat, or the result of some complex, esoteric load calculation; it is simply the width of the railroad tracks in England. And it was English expatriates who built the U.S. railroad.

Now why did the Brits lay their railroad tracks 4' 8½" apart? Because they built the tracks over the old tramway tracks, which were laid at that spacing. And the tramway tracks were built to fit, of course, the tramway carts. That's because the carts were built in the same shops and on the same jigs as were the carriages. The British carriages all had their wheels set 4' 8½" apart, because if they didn't, they would not fit in the spacing of wheel ruts already established throughout the English countryside. (Hang on, we're getting close.) These wheel ruts were very old; in fact, they were there since the Romans rolled into town and built access roads for their legions of army troops. The jeep of the Roman army was the imperial war chariot, which featured a wheel spacing of 4' 8½". This happens to be just wide enough to accommodate — you guessed it — the width of two imperial warhorse butts. So now you know what horse's ass designed the space shuttle.

This story, which is widely held true in the carriage trade, by the way, expresses one of my most fundamental lessons of the trade: You don't need measurements to build things out of wood. It is a lesson that has changed the way I set up machines, the way I lay out cut lines and, in fact, the entire way in which I think about the woodworking process from concept through construction.

To explain myself, let's go back to the carriage makers of merry old England. When they needed to lay out the hub spacing on a length of axle, they didn't go out to the stable, stand directly behind a horse and spread out their arms to either side while holding a tape measure. You wouldn't do that either, would you? Besides, tape measures weren't invented yet. And besides again, they didn't need to know a numbered dimension, because woodworkers of that era didn't work exclusively, if at all, to numbers.

It's likely, in fact, that none of the carriage makers knew that the hubs of the axles they were building were set 4' 8½" apart. They probably didn't know the dimension number of any other part of the chariot either. That's because they didn't need to. Instead, these coach-wrights, like other preindustrial-age tradesmen, generally built to story sticks and pattern templates. As my experience and confidence deepen with the years, I have taken more to working without numbers as well. There are pieces of furniture in my portfolio that I have never known how tall, wide or deep they are. I once built a cosmetic cabinet that was inspired by, and completely driven by, a short piece of wide pine board that had an unusual grain pattern on its face. To turn the board into a door panel, I cut it to a length and width that centered the pattern. To determine the width of the framework that would surround it to turn it into a door, I held various sample widths of frame stock against the panel until the visual weight seemed right. The depth of the cabinet was determined by the largest perfume bottle that would have to fit inside it.

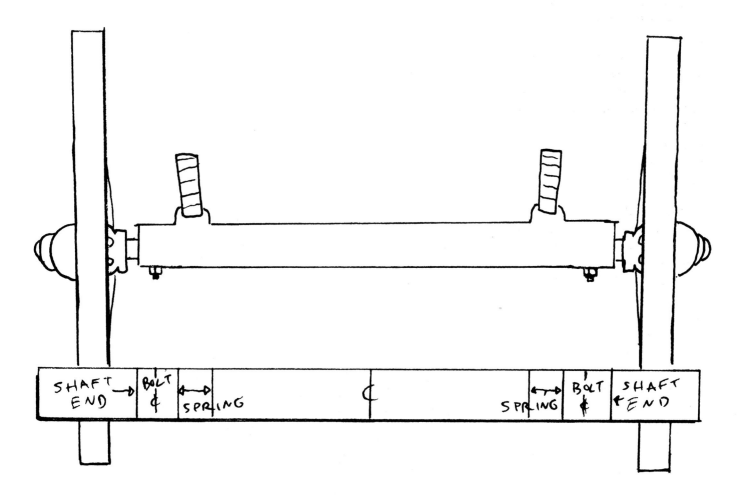

All these dimensions were recorded not as numbers, but as ticks on a stick — a story stick as it is traditionally called. Notches on a story stick probably recorded the carriage wheel hub positions for the coachwrights. I won't say that I build every project this way. While I often design without numbers, I do take off numbered dimensions of components from my full-scale drawings to make up cutting lists. That's because my primary cutting machines (and I do use machines when I'm trying to make a living at woodworking) have indexed fences. I read the number off the cut list, set the fence and go. A board cut 8" wide according to the table saw's rip fence cursor index will exactly match a strip of wood cut 8" long according to the cursor index of the miter saw's sliding stop. It doesn't get much faster or easier than this for production work.

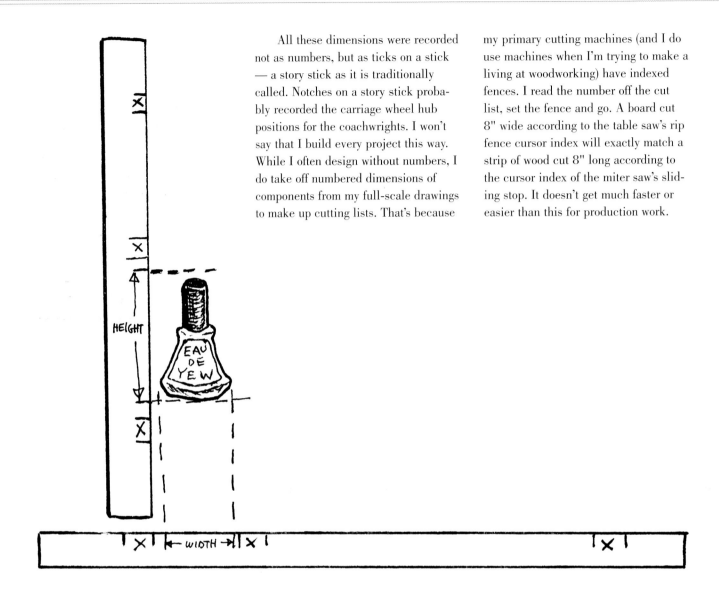

MEDICINE CABINET STORY STICK

Story sticks do, however, play a large role in my woodworking processes — even in production kitchen cabinet work. As I've explained in detail in my book *Building Traditional Kitchen Cabinets,* I use story sticks to record the location of everything from walls, to windows, to pet doors and to outlets in the area in which the cabinets will be installed. Back in the shop, the stick acts as a two-dimensional representation of that room, telling the whole story of what goes where. To determine the size and spacing of the cabinets to be built for that space, I mark their positions right on the stick, right down to the size of rails and stiles, drawer faces and doors. When the proportions and functions look right, then I'll whip out the tape measure and get numbered dimensions for my cutting lists.

KITCHEN STORY STICK

I've also gotten into the habit of using story sticks in lieu of measurements whenever dead-on accuracy is critical. Locating the attachment holes for a piece of hardware is one good example. When I try to use numbers to transfer dimensions accurately I often find myself fudging them a bit because of my lately developed inability to read divisions much finer than 1/32" — or to even remember the fractions long enough to make the transfer on those days when I forget to drink my ginseng tea. The story stick is a work of nonfiction. It tells the truth, the whole truth and nothing but the truth.

TEMPLATE (SCRAP OF ¼" PLYWOOD)

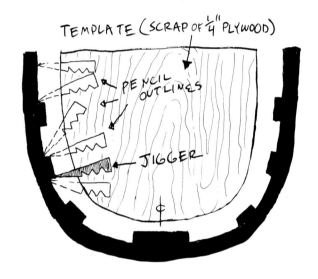

PENCIL OUTLINES

JIGGER

PLYWOOD STOCK

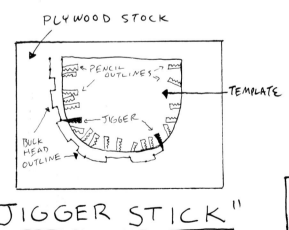

PENCIL OUTLINES

JIGGER

TEMPLATE

BULK HEAD OUTLINE

" JIGGER STICK "

PROBLEM — FITTING PLYWOOD BULKHEAD TO CURVE OF BOAT HULL

SOLUTION — JIGGER STICK™

① TEMPORARILY RIG SCRAP OF PLYWOOD IN SPACE

② MAKE A JIGGER STICK™ :
 — ¼" TO ½" THICK WOOD ABOUT 12" LONG

③ PLACE JIGGER STICK SO POINT TOUCHES "BENCH MARK" POINT ON HULL, THEN TRACE OUTLINE OF JIGGER WHERE IT RESTS ON SCRAP

④ AFTER ALL BENCH MARKS ESTABLISHED (THE MORE COMPLEX THE CURVES AND CORNERS, THE MORE YOU NEED) REMOVE TEMPLATE AND TAPE ONTO BULKHEAD STOCK

⑤ SET JIGGER ON OUTLINES AND TRANSFER BENCHMARK POINTS TO STOCK. CONNECT DOTS, THEN CUT BULKHEAD

JIGGER STICK BEST USED IN SITUATIONS WHERE MEETING EDGES ARE CURVED AND/OR HIGHLY COMPLEX

A scrap of tar paper and a chunk of scrap wood compose one of the most precise layout tools available to a woodworker.

When one of my earliest mentors in woodworking, the late boatbuilder Bud McIntosh of Dover, New Hampshire, showed me a couple of his favorite layout tricks I was impressed, but I wasn't happy. I wanted to see tricks that would show me how to use all my brand-new rulers and squares, my antique dividers and my other precision layout devices (including some that I wasn't all that sure just what it was that they did). I didn't really want to see Bud perform his "Joe Frogger" and "Jigger Stick" tricks with some offcuts picked up off the shop floor and a strip of ratty tar paper, tricks that would keep all my lovely tool candy in the toolbox!

But he did, and my fancy tools have yet to outdo his methods for recording the cutting line point positions of even the most complex fitting situations. You can find more information about these shop-made, scrap-wood tools in my book *Built-In Furniture*.

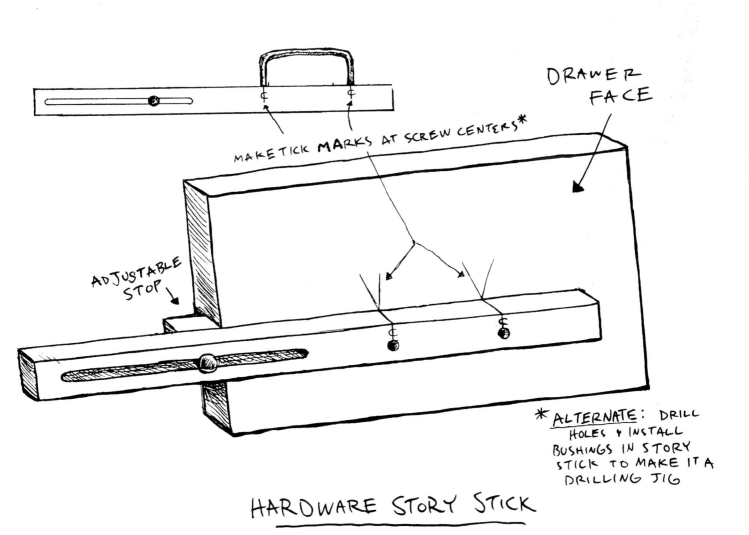

DRAWER FACE

MAKE TICK MARKS AT SCREW CENTERS*

ADJUSTABLE STOP

* ALTERNATE: DRILL HOLES & INSTALL BUSHINGS IN STORY STICK TO MAKE IT A DRILLING JIG

HARDWARE STORY STICK

☐ - FROG

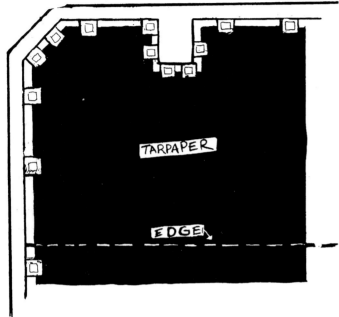

TARPAPER

EDGE

* FROG - 1½" SQUARE
BLOCK

JOE FROGGER

PROBLEM : FITTING PLYWOOD INTO
COMPLEX CORNER AREA
SOLUTION : JOE FROGGER™

① CUT PIECE OF TARPAPER TO
ROUGH SHAPE OF CORNER AREA,
TAPE TO FLOOR

② MAKE FROG AS SHOWN*— MUST
BE PERFECTLY SQUARE!

③ HOLD ONE EDGE OF FROG
AGAINST WALL AND MARK
OPPOSITE EDGE ON TARPAPER
REPEAT IN MULTIPLE PLACES ALONG
RUN

④ REMOVE PAPER FROM FLOOR. TAPE
ONTO PLYWOOD TO BE CUT.

⑤ USE FROG TO TRANSFER MEETING
EDGE LOCATIONS ONTO PLYWOOD

JOE FROGGER™ BEST USED IN
SITUATIONS WHERE MEETING
EDGES ARE RELATIVELY STRAIGHT

Just because wood just lies there doesn't mean it's dead.

Wood, unlike most other raw materials that other types of artisans get to work with, has a life after death — and that isn't always a good thing. With plywood you can usually tell if you are going to have trouble; if the sheet is warped, then any piece you cut from it will be, too (at least to some extent). What you see is what you get. But with solid wood you can't always be so sure. (Plywood is made up of solid wood, of course, but in layers too thin to create large dynamic effects.) In other words, boards can still change in dimension and shape depending on, and in response to, environmental conditions in both its past and its present. Pretty spooky if you think about it.

Usually, we can compensate for dimensional changes as I talked about earlier. However, changes in shape — twisting and cupping — are harder to deal with structurally. They can overpower framework systems and fastening strategies and throw the entire assembly out of kilter. It's much better to nip these potential problems in the bud during the milling process.

The first line of defense is to know the wood you are using. First, you must be sure the wood is properly seasoned. That means checking to be sure that its moisture content is within a few percentage points of the average environment it will live in during its functional lifetime. I use a pin-type resistance meter. The next thing to know is the characteristics of its species. Here we are concerned especially with its specific gravity. The higher this value, the denser the wood is and the more likely it will move around with moisture changes in its environment. This information is readily available in a number of books and government pamphlets.

Next, know the boards themselves. Look at their grain patterns carefully. If you see complex grain patterns that swirl and whirl and run off the face of the board in places (rather than running from end to end), then you know that this board probably came from a very active and stressed part of the tree. Wood taken from near the root bulge, from near the base or branches, or from branches themselves are full of stresses that have been locked into the grain of the wood. This dynamic wood is rarely complacent; it does not like to stay flat when shaped into boards. It's a challenge, because highly patterned grain often creates the most interesting and attractive board stock. This is why stressed wood was traditionally used mostly as veneer stock; it was stable because it was so thin and adhered to a backing of stable, flat wood.

Test this life-after-death theory for yourself by running a particularly squirrelly board through the flattening/squaring process and then setting it aside for a few weeks. Chances are (especially if there have been dramatic weather changes in your corner of the world) that when you lay that board on a nice flat table surface like a table saw it's going to rock anywhere from a little bit to a lotta bit. That wood was just another pretty face with a checkered past.

ALONG EDGE OF BOARD

LOOK FOR GRAIN RUNNING OUT OF PARALLEL TO SURFACES. THE CLOSER TOGETHER IT EXITS ON OPPOSITE SURFACES, THE MORE UNSTABLE AND WEAK IT MAY BE.

AT THE ENDS OF THE BOARD

IT'S BAD IF:

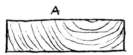

A

BOARD HAS BOTH RADIAL + TANGENTIAL GRAIN (WHICH CAN CAUSE WARPING)

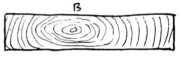

B

CENTER OF TREE IS CAPTURED IN BOARD (CHECKING MAY OCCUR)

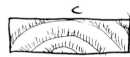

C

WIDE GROWTH RINGS (MAKES BOARD BOTH WEAK AND SUBJECT TO LARGE DIMENSION CHANGES

ON SURFACES

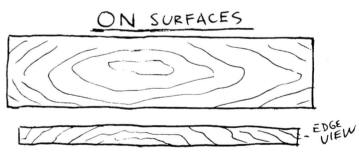

EDGE VIEW

GRAIN WITH OVAL PATTERNS MEANS GRAIN EXITS SURFACE IN TWO DIRECTIONS, MAKES PLANING DIFFICULT AND BOARD MAY CUP LENGTHWISE.

74

The surface planer is not the right tool to make a board flat.

When you make assemblies of rectilinear components (i.e., boxes as opposed to free-form carving), you must use boards and pieces of sheet stock that are also rectilinear and will stay that way as closely as possible. Otherwise, your nice boxes may turn into free-form carvings (which is all right if your mother allows you to do pure art and you don't care if things like doors and drawers actually work like most people expect them to). I've already talked about how to account for wood movement in the design phase and how to

choose plywood and solid wood to lessen the chance of the wood moving in the first place. Now it's time to talk about how to get a board flat and square to its edges in the milling process — a process that is rarely taught correctly in my experience.

In high school shop I was taught to square up a board by first running it through the surface planer on both sides and to then take it over to the jointer where I would joint each edge square to the face. The problem with this method is that while you may get both faces flat and parallel to one another, there is no assurance that those parallel faces will be straight. The surface planer has a very short bed and therefore could care less if the board is curved along its length.

EFFECT OF DOUBLE-SIDED SURFACING

IF PLANER BED IS SHORT RELATIVE TO LENGTH OF BOARD, IT HAS NO WAY OF "KNOWING" THAT THE BOARD IS CURVED OVER IT'S LENGTH.

THUS WHILE THE TOP OF THE BOARD WILL BE SURFACED PARALLEL (SIDE TO SIDE) TO THE BOTTOM SURFACE, IT WILL FOLLOW ANY LENGTHWISE CURVE.

Could you solve the straightness problem by running both faces over a wide jointer with a long bed? Well, no. The faces will be flat and they will be straight, but there is absolutely no control over whether they are parallel to one another. So here's what I do: I run one face through the jointer, being careful not to press the board down very hard with my pressure pads; I just let the machine cut away the high spots first. (If I press too hard, the board will spring back to the warp still lurking within.) This face, which is now flat and straight, serves as the reference surface for all subsequent millwork.

The next millwork step is to get the other face flat. I can now go to the sur-face planer because I already have a straight and flat reference surface to run over the planer's bed. After I get the top surface completely flat, I can then plane down to the desired thickness. I try to remove about the same amount of material from each face so I maintain even moisture content levels around the center line of the board — a way to minimize shape changes. Once the board is surfaced to the specified thickness, I take it to the jointer and joint one edge (usually the one that is roughly concave). To ensure the opposite edge will be parallel, I rip the stock to width plus about $\frac{1}{16}$", then joint the sawn edge smooth and square. The result is a truly squared-up piece of wood.

EFFECT OF DOUBLE-SIDED JOINING

IF BOTH SURFACES ARE JOINTED, THE BOARD MAY BE FLAT CROSSWISE AND STRAIGHT LENGTHWISE, BUT THERE IS NO CONTROL OVER MAKING THE SURFACES PARALLEL TO ONE ANOTHER.

SOLUTION: JOINT ONE FACE, THEN SURFACE THE OPPOSITE.

A hand plane can outperform a power jointer — even if it doesn't get the edges square!

If I need to join the edges of two boards perfectly to one another, I don't try to do it by jointing each one separately on my 8" power jointer. It does a good job, but it does not do a perfect job (especially on long stock) because I am not a perfect helper. To be one, I would need to maintain precisely even support on both the infeed and outfeed portions of the stock, and I have yet to get really good at that. So instead, I clamp both boards together in a vise with the edges to be joined facing up, good faces facing in. I then run my freshly sharpened and aligned 22" hand jointer plane down their length, taking an even shaving off both edges at the same time. It usually takes only three to four passes, less than a minute, and the boards are ready for joining. The really cool thing is: I don't have to worry about making the edges perfectly square to the face of the board. That's because when you bookmatch the boards, any variation from square is canceled out. It's foolproof, which is something I can really appreciate!

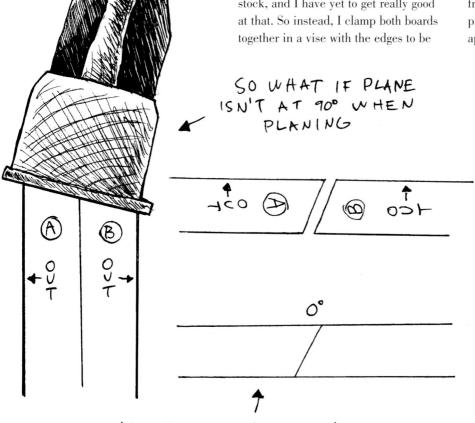

SO WHAT IF PLANE
ISN'T AT 90° WHEN
PLANING

WHEN JOINED, THE OFF-ANGLES
ARE COMPLIMENTARY AND THUS CANCEL
OUT TO PRODUCE 0°

HAND JOINTING EDGES

Ripping is not the only way to make a board narrower, and sometimes it's not even the right way.

When I lived in Pennsylvania, an Appalachian furniture maker I met on the craft fair circuit gave me this mystery to solve: Back near the turn of the 19th century, the new fire chief of Cumberland, Maryland, decided to replace one of the station's old and fire-singed wood ladders. Seeing he could obtain the ladder quicker and at a better price by ordering it from a commercial outfit in Philadelphia rather than hiring the job out to the usual supplier, an old orchard ladder maker who lived way back up a West Virginia hollow, he requisitioned the funds and made the purchase. When he brought the new ladder into the firehouse, the fireman's captain took one quick look at the ladder and said he would not set foot on it if his life depended on it — which, of course, it did in his line of work. The surprised chief looked closely at the ladder. The side rails were made of full-length, defect-free white oak heartwood and the rungs were made of perfectly clear, hickory heartwood. All the joints were well done and securely fastened. Why, then, did the captain so vehemently reject the chief's purchase?

The answer, as the Appalachian artisan was happy to point out to this dumbfounded young New Englander who was calling himself a woodworker, was summed up in two words: sawn rungs. The captain could tell by looking at the grain that the rungs had been ripped from a board rather than split and shaved from a wedge of green wood.

That was the ladder's fatal flaw. The power saw, no more than its operator, could care less if the grain of the board ran parallel to the length of the rung. The captain knew that the strength of a rung is directly proportional to the percentage of grain (or, to be technical, the cellulose fibers) that runs full length from rail to rail. If more than 20 percent

of those fibers exit the rung before they reach the rails, that rung, under the load of a fully outfitted fireman and the damsel in distress slung over his shoulder, would very likely fail. The chief should have known better, as should this woodworker.

SAWN RUNG

SPLIT RUNG

IF LESS THAN 20% OF THE ANNUAL RINGS MAKE IT FROM ONE END OF THE RUNG TO THE OTHER, IT IS LIKELY TO BREAK UNDER SUDDEN, HEAVY LOADS.

IF MOST OF THE GRAIN RUNS PARALLEL TO THE LENGTH OF THE RUNG, IT WILL BE MORE ABLE AND LIKELY TO WITHSTAND HEAVY LOADS.

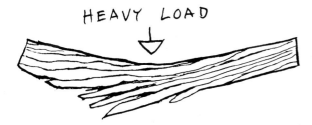

HEAVY LOAD

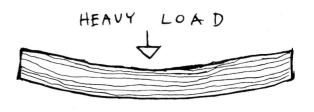

HEAVY LOAD

SAWN VERSUS SPLIT RUNG STOCK

Ripping can be one of the slowest ways to make a board narrow.

You might deduce from this and the last secret that I don't like ripping much. Well, I probably do have a prejudice against it, because when I did timber framing in the mid-1970s I did a lot of ripping with a handsaw. When working with those huge summer beams and girters, many times our big circular saws still wouldn't cut deep enough to complete the joints. It wouldn't have been all that bad, but I was a greenhorn and didn't know that you had to hone the teeth nearly daily if you wanted to keep a hand ripsaw working to its potential. I did learn to keep spraying kerosene on the blade, and that helped some. I also eventually learned to hold the ripsaw correctly when cutting — nearly upright rather than at the 45° I was used to holding handsaws when crosscutting.

Of course, I opted for the powered circular saw (we called them Skilsaws back then when we were reckless and didn't pay heed to trademark law) every chance I got. I was pretty fast at ripping with my Milwaukee 7" screamer, almost as fast as some old-time, down east boatbuilders whom I used to watch rip dory planks out of pine planks by hand with their ancient ripsaws. Someday when I grow up I hope I'll be that skilled and that strong.

But why rip at all when you can split? Back in the mid-1970s, under the tutelage of Vermont chairmaker David Sawyer, I learned to make farm implements and chairs from green wood. I'll never forget my amazement at first seeing David produce a 4'-long, nearly hexagonal chunk of white oak the size of

my wrist from a tree stump in less than a minute with only minimal effort. I'm still amazed today when I look at the Pacific North Coast Indian longhouses, which feature walls fashioned from huge, uniformly sized planks of cedar that never saw the teeth of any saw. At some Canadian museums, one can observe native craftsmen demonstrating the aboriginal house-building technology of wedging planks out of logs. The only sound is the clump of wood on wood — not the scream of an electric motor and its spinning metal teeth. The only smell is the sweet aroma of cedar shavings — not the acrid, irritating dust spit out by a hot, spinning cutting blade. And the speed at which they get these planks to emerge from the huge parent logs is almost breathtaking. It's almost enough to make me want to build houses again, at least those kinds of houses with those kinds of tools.

Power isn't always necessary or appropriate to make fast, accurate crosscuts.

I wish I could tell you differently, but just because you finally own a big, beautiful stationary power tool doesn't mean you have to use it all the time. I've spent several hours building a miniature crosscut sled that could carry the tiniest pieces of stock (such as furniture trim mouldings) through the blade of my 3 hp, 10" stationary saw. It works great, but, in fact, it's overkill for anything but major production runs. I

already had on hand the simplest jig you can imagine that works impeccably well to guide my fine-tooth handsaw through a variety of crosscuts. With this jig and handsaw setup, I can cut $\frac{1}{4}$"-thick mouldings in three strokes. I could make a couple of dozen crosscuts in the time it would take me to change the blade on the table saw, set the height and angle of the arbor and install and check the crosscut sled.

Admittedly, one advantage of a powered blade over a handsaw is that you can make tiny end cuts to trim the length to a perfect fit. A handsaw needs a kerf to ride in to make an accurate cut. Unfortunately, power saws often get a little greedy when you use them to eat away at the end of stick of wood. So what I do, which has led to far less whining on my part about miscuts, is to hit the end of the cut with a sanding block (for tiny stock) or a block plane to achieve that final, perfect fit.

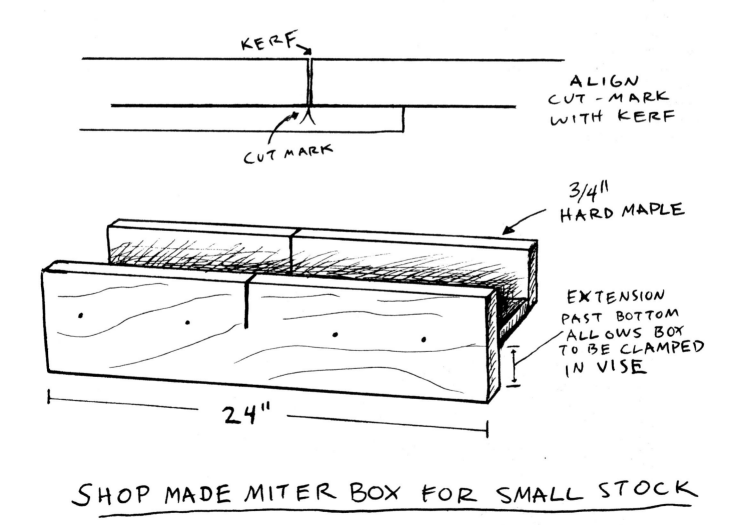

KERF

ALIGN
CUT-MARK
WITH KERF

CUT MARK

3/4" HARD MAPLE

EXTENSION
PAST BOTTOM
ALLOWS BOX
TO BE CLAMPED
IN VISE

24"

SHOP MADE MITER BOX FOR SMALL STOCK

When power shaping, it's sometimes a good idea to cut the wrong way before cutting the right way.

Talk about learning through the school of hard knocks: When I was woefully unaware of the downhill rule of routing and shaping, I made some horrible (read *expensive*) mistakes. These mistakes meant hours of time recutting and remilling components. The problem was exacerbated by the fact that I was, at the time, working with two woods that love to fracture along their grain lines: oak and fir.

The downhill rule is rarely taught in the tool's standard operating manual because it can be dangerous. That's because going downhill means feeding the stock into the cutters in the same

direction they are spinning, which means the cutters can grab the stock and fling it across the room. Not a good thing. But the good thing about going downhill is that fracturing and tear-out are greatly minimized.

To minimize the danger, you must take certain precautions. First, you must use fixtures that hold the wood firmly against the table and fence. These can be the same fixtures you use when feeding the stock normally. I use shop-made featherboards, commercial wheeled hold-downs or a small power feeder. Second, you must set the height of the cutter and/or the position of the fence so

the cutter will remove only a small amount of material; I never cut more than ⅛" on the first downhill cut. Depending on the shape being cut and on the propensity of the stock to fracture, you may need to run downhill only on the first cut anyway. I can usually tell by the smoothness and even the sound of the downhill cut if I can switch to the standard uphill cutting direction for the balance of the cut. Finally, you must make sure that no one that you like or owes you money is in the potential line of fire if the stock should get away from you.

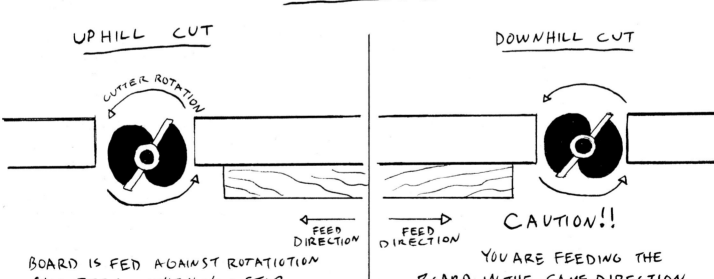

MILLING THE HILL

UPHILL CUT

CUTTER ROTATION

FEED DIRECTION

BOARD IS FED AGAINST ROTATIOTION OF CUTTER. WHEN YOU STOP PUSHING, THE BLADES STOP CUTTING — WHICH IS SAFE — BUT CAN LEAD TO ROUGH CUTS.

DOWNHILL CUT

FEED DIRECTION

CAUTION!!

YOU ARE FEEDING THE BOARD IN THE SAME DIRECTION THE BLADES ARE SPINNING. IF YOU STOP PUSHING, THE CUTTERS MAY KEEP PULLING THE BOARD FORWARD. GOOD FOR FIRST SHALLOW PASS TO ENSURE SMOOTH CUT.

Holes aren't always, and don't always need to be, round.

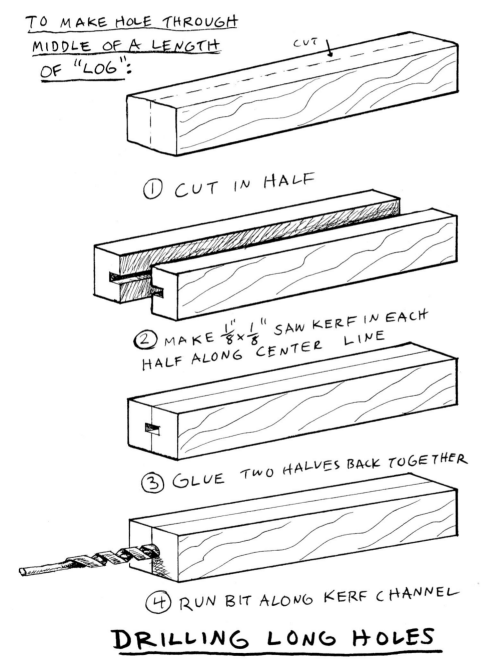

TO MAKE HOLE THROUGH MIDDLE OF A LENGTH OF "LOG":

CUT

① CUT IN HALF

② MAKE ⅛" × ⅛" SAW KERF IN EACH HALF ALONG CENTER LINE

③ GLUE TWO HALVES BACK TOGETHER

④ RUN BIT ALONG KERF CHANNEL

DRILLING LONG HOLES

A number of Christmases back, I decided to build my sweetheart a table lamp that would feature a solid walnut base and a shade woven from clear pine shavings. Since this was a Christmas present I didn't start making it until, of course, December 23. Things were going smoothly until it was time to cut the hole through the 18"-long chunk of walnut for the lamp cord. Rifling through my tool drawers, I could not find my long ship augers anywhere — probably because I had loaned them to my shop partner who had taken them to the other side of the state for the month. Now how was Santa's elf going to make an 18"-long hole without a drill bit?

That was the Zen koan that sparked this Christmas Eve revelation: A hole is an opening through something. No one (including Webster's Dictionary) ever said anything about it being round. This meant that since I didn't need the hole to be round, I didn't necessarily need a drill bit to make it. So I started thinking of other ways to make a hole — a passageway through this particular chunk of wood. That's when I remembered Bud McIntosh showing me how he drilled the long (we're talking 3' or more) hole for the prop shaft in a chunk of locust. The secret was to first rip the shaft log in half and then make a saw kerf down the center of each half. When you bolted the two halves back together, you presented yourself with a little channel that ran from the center of one end of the log to the other — a perfect pilot hole to guide the worm of the ship auger. Now, I thought to myself, if I simply made the saw kerf a little bigger with a dado blade, I would have my hole for the lamp cord — which is just what I did and just what I got.

joining, bending and smoothing

LESSON FIFTY-ONE

When you need a big piece of wood, it's sometimes better to make it yourself rather than to let Mother Nature make it for you.

If you are making posts and beams for a timber-framed shelter or making dead wood to form the keel of a boat, you definitely need big wood — often the longer and bulkier the better. In these situations, you don't want to compromise the strength or water resistance of the structure by cobbling together more pieces than necessary.

There is, however, one problem inherent to wood of all species that must be accounted for: the greater the volume of wood, the more it can change size and shape (with changes in ambient moisture levels). This is generally not a problem in timber frames or boat keels as the amount of movement is small relative to the overall scale of these massive assemblies.

DEADWOOD IS BIGWOOD.

Furniture is another story, however. Here, even small amounts of movement may be noticeable or even damaging because of the close tolerances within joints and between components. For this reason, I generally shy away from using big chunks of wood when I need to meet a design requirement calling for bulky-looking parts. A good example is shown in the drawing. Here, the legs of this cherry wood, Craftsman-style dining table needed to be almost 4" thick to look right. I could easily have made them from a 4×4 or two 2×4s glued together, but I would have run the risk of having this large mass of wood change shape during the life of this table. I worried that the legs might twist and/or pull away from the apron joints. So instead I made up the legs from four pieces of wood, mitering them together at the corners. The miters completely hide the fact that the leg is a hollow composite. Another plus is that I can use face grain on all four sides of the leg — a trick that makes the legs a little more interesting looking.

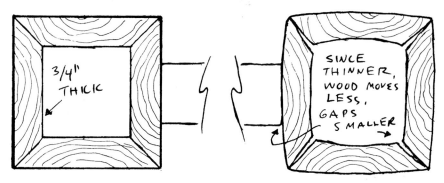

CROSS SECTIONS OF 4/4 TABLE LEGS

1 1/2" THICK

GAP

GLUE FAILURE*

RIDGE

THICK PIECES OF HARDWOOD TEND TO CUP (AWAY FROM HEART) WHEN DRYING, CAUSING DISTORTIONS AND RIDGE LINES AT JOINTS.
* IF GLUE DOESN'T FAIL DURING SHRINKAGE, SOMETHING ELSE MUST GIVE - USUALLY ASSEMBLY WILL TWIST.

3/4" THICK

SINCE THINNER, WOOD MOVES LESS, GAPS SMALLER

THINNER PIECES ARE LESS PRONE TO MOVEMENT. IN THIS CASE ALL 4 PIECES TEND TO TIGHTEN WHEN SHRINKING, KEEPING JOINTS INVISIBLE.
NOTE: ALWAYS ORIENT BOARDS HEART-SIDE FACING OUT.

TABLE LEG OPTIONS

An overfit joint doesn't make a fitter joint.

When I was first starting out in woodworking I would go to great lengths to make my joints fit perfectly. For example, when making the shoulders of tenons for a mortise-and-tenon joint, I would spent a lot of time trying to get those shoulders to fit perfectly everywhere against the cheek of the mating surface. It was a nice exercise in chisel and shoulder plane work, but other than that it was a complete waste of time.

The fact is, tenon shoulders don't need to fit flush to a cheek; only the outer edge area of the shoulder needs to do that. I undercut the shoulder so it doesn't get in the way and to speed up the fitting process (since I have to trim only the $\frac{1}{8}$" or so that is making contact with the mating surface). I can get away with this because the shoulder connection is not where a mortise and tenon gets its strength. The outside of the shoulder must fit perfectly (for looks and to help the joint maintain its angles), but there is no functional reason for the rest of the shoulder to touch the cheek. The strength of the joint comes from the physical connection between the face of the tenon and the cheeks of the mortise with the additional locking action of glue or, better, a peg or wedge. The quality of my joinery would have been much better served if I had devoted my energy to more closely matching the tenons to their mortise holes.

Even then, there is no need for a perfect match; in fact, some looseness is needed to ensure that the joint doesn't jam during assembly if water-based glue is used (which might expand the tenon) or that the joint doesn't become too tight if the mortise holes shrink a little. The trick is to learn just how much slop to leave. That's another thing I should have been focusing on instead of making perfect shoulders.

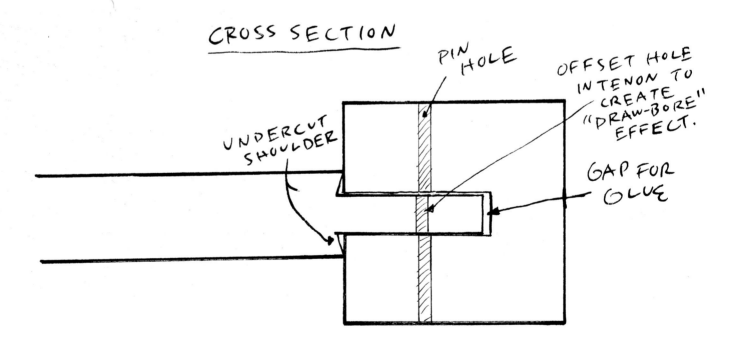

CROSS SECTION

PIN HOLE

OFFSET HOLE IN TENON TO CREATE "DRAW-BORE" EFFECT.

UNDERCUT SHOULDER

GAP FOR GLUE

ANATOMY OF A MORTISE AND TENON JOINT

Always work with a third hand.

Just yesterday I was down in the shop doing a little joinery — trimming cabinet door-frame tenons to fit their mortises. After the fourth one, I noticed I was getting a little fatigued and frustrated with my progress. I then noticed what I was doing wrong. By not bothering to clamp the frame, I was making my body do all the work. With one hand having to hold and keep the piece from moving (even with the help of a bench hook), my other hand had to take care of the chiseling on its own. To ensure accuracy when using a chisel aggressively, you need both hands. So here was yet another lesson for me in the counterproductiveness of laziness.

Clamps are our friends. They are our willing and able, if somewhat passive, third hands. They may take a little time to set up and take down, but they ultimately make the work itself go faster by allowing our other two hands to do what they do best — which is working the tools.

If you have a choice, make the work come to you.

I was reminded of yet another lesson in the shop that day. Crawling under the partially built gypsy wagon to notch a joist for a porch support, I kept kicking myself. Not because I'm that spastic, but because I knew I should have made that notch a long time ago. Long enough ago that the joist would not have yet become a permanent part of the wagon, but instead still be a nice, passive piece of wood that I could lay on my work bench at a comfortable working height.

This is an extreme example, but the rule of bringing the work to you holds true throughout many typical processes. For example, when I build framed doors I will go so far as to cut the hinge and latch mortises before I assemble the door itself. In this way, I can clamp the stile securely and at the most comfortable height — generally a difficult thing to do when the stile is part of the door. I'm always striving to think ahead so that I can avoid putting myself in an awkward position to do any type of milling or carving process.

The absolute strongest bends in components are made without bending the wood.

Sawing to a curve, making a series of closely spaced kerfs, laminating thin strips and steaming the wood to make it pliable are all viable ways of getting wood to change direction over its length. While each of these methods has its pros and cons and most appropriate applications, they share one thing in common: all depend on the woodworker to make the wood go around the corner.

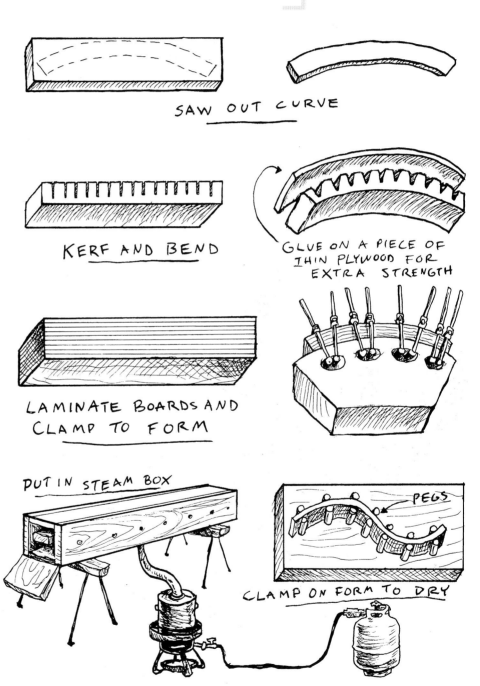

SAW OUT CURVE

KERF AND BEND

GLUE ON A PIECE OF THIN PLYWOOD FOR EXTRA STRENGTH

LAMINATE BOARDS AND CLAMP TO FORM

PUT IN STEAM BOX

PEGS

CLAMP ON FORM TO DRY

89

That's not necessarily a bad thing, but if you want the strongest bend, a bend that has the least chance of ever failing under a heavy load and adverse environmental conditions, a bend that looks right because all the grain says it's right, then there's one more choice: go to the source. Go to where the bend has already been made for you by the tree itself. You can likely find the bend you want at the base of large branches or at the butt of the tree where the roots begin to spread out. Previous generations of woodworkers commonly used these areas of the tree (called crooks) to make such things as boat keels and the huge corbels of cathedral-size timber frames.

You don't need any special machines to turn crooks into corbels. For countless centuries it's been done with hatchets and drawknives. These days, however, we can opt for resaw-type band saws that make that work go really quickly. Since you are working with wood without well-defined reference surfaces (as opposed to boards), it is important to use a sturdy carriage system to carry the rough crook through the blade during the initial ripping process. After that you can cut the outside and inside curves with a narrower blade installed on the same band saw. For the absolute strongest bend, however, strive to make the curved cuts as close as possible to the natural curve of the grain.

PLANK SAWN OUT OF BEND
IN BRANCH OR TRUNK

NOTE HOW GRAIN FOLLOWS
CURVE OF STEM

SAWING A STEM OUT OF A CROOK

Smoothing wood with sandpaper isn't the fastest way to make wood smooth.

Sanding isn't the most pleasant experience either. To see what I'm talking about, try this little experiment. With a freshly sharpened smoothing plane set for a very fine cut, take a couple of strokes across the surface of a small piece of hardwood; cherry or walnut would be a good choice. Now turn the piece over and sand the opposite face with a progression of grits of sandpaper, starting with 120 if the surface is relatively clean and flat to begin with. Go all the way up to 320. Now, using a scrap of wet-and-dry 400-grit paper, rub

a little oil into the wood on both surfaces, using the paper as an applicator. Look at and feel both sides; they are almost identical in smoothness and luster. The only difference is, you got the planed surface to this point in about one-quarter the time it took you on the sanded side.

While I've certainly put in my time with orbital sanders — they are indispensable for certain production applications in cabinetmaking — I now give equal time to smooth planing when I'm furniture making. In building my last

project, a cherry wood dining table, I didn't use sandpaper of any grit less than 320 — and that was during the finishing process. Instead, I surfaced all the components (usually before assembly) with my trusty Lie-Nielsen smoothing plane. In areas of cross grain I chased the plane with a cabinet scraper. The resulting surface is every bit as smooth as one I would have achieved with much more time listening to, and sucking dust from, an orbital sander. The only difference is that you can feel the difference between this planed surface and a sanded surface — which is not a bad thing and which brings us to the next secret.

Every finished surface need not be perfectly flat or smooth.

Prior to my experimenting with planed versus sanded finishes, I used to think that in order for a surface to be finished it needed to be baby-butt smooth and flat as, well, a board. I've since realized through exposure to the woodworking of other cultures that you can have smoothness without the flatness. You can have a finished surface that is not even close to flat but is, instead, textured. These days, my planed surfaces look flat, but they don't feel flat. Anyone with a sensitive hand can feel the subtle ruffles left behind by the gently curved plane blade.

If the texture can be seen, it literally becomes the surface. So instead of being locked into my old cabinetmaker's mind-set of *flat* equals *finished*, I now allow my design storming sessions to explore finished surfaces that move beyond the two-dimensional. I now see that adding a third dimension brings more senses into play to experience and to appreciate the piece of work. If I use plant oils for finishing, I invoke yet another dimension, the sense of smell. As far as I'm concerned, the more senses that can be involved, the better my chances get to make the project exciting, fulfilling and successful.

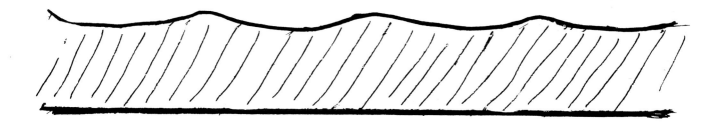

SCALLOPS LEFT BEHIND BY CURVED PLANE BLADE

The best time to put together an assembly is near the beginning, not the end of the process.

One of the worst experiences a wood-worker can have is the moment when he finds out what it means to have a whole not equal the sum of its parts. That is a moment I personally have experienced and not forgotten (no matter how hard I've tried).

What happened was this: I was building a small, pentagonal-shaped coffee table from koa wood (a beautiful but pricey Hawaiian hardwood) and had reached the stage where all the parts were cut and shaped and joints made. With a little final trimming I made sure that each apron-to-leg joint fit perfectly — tight shoulders all around, proper meeting angles and so on. Proud of myself for going that extra mile, I got out the band clamps, clamping pads and glue. Working my way around the table, I applied yellow glue to the joints and hand-pressed them together. When I reached the last joint I would be ready to throw the band clamps over the whole assembly and draw the five aprons home into the five legs.

Well, it didn't happen. The last joint was so far out of alignment that no amount of clamping and cussing would persuade it to close up — unless at least two other joints opened up. Worse still, the glue was starting to set up. I was now experiencing firsthand what happens when the whole does not equal the sum of its parts. At least I learned my lesson. From that day on, well before I even begin to think about glue, I dry assemble the entire piece with all the clamps and pressure that will be used in the wet run.

A dry run not only ensures that all the joints will fit, but it also gives me a good idea of how to best sequence the gluing and clamping process. It also shows me how to place and sequence the fasteners and may even show what parts would best be prefinished prior to assembly. For these reasons, dry assembly now comes as early as possible in my construction flowchart. A nice bonus is that I get a sneak preview of what the finished piece is going to look like. Yet another bonus is that I don't have to figure out what to do with a bunch of koa wood with sawn-off ends.

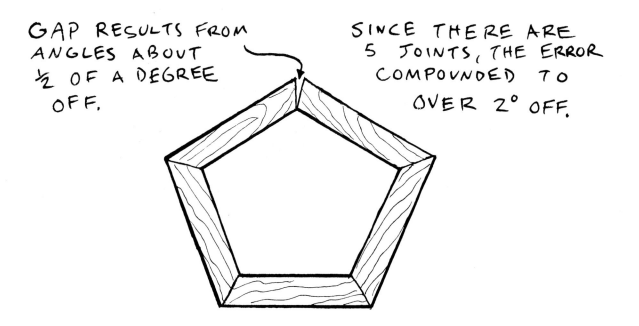

GAP RESULTS FROM ANGLES ABOUT ½ OF A DEGREE OFF.

SINCE THERE ARE 5 JOINTS, THE ERROR COMPOUNDED TO OVER 2° OFF.

A MISS-CUT AT THE PENTAGON

Some of the best clamps in life are free.

Having done some boatbuilding over the course of the last three decades, I was endowed (as are most boatbuilders) with a rack full of C-clamps. I have found plenty of use for them outside of boat-building, and there were times when I was grateful for every last one of them. In some ways, though, their abiding presence has long put off an important discovery: C-clamps suck.

Their small heads pinpoint the huge pressure that these clamps can exert, creating dimples in the workpiece unless you manage to get pads in between the heads and the wood. That trick takes at least three hands: one to hold the clamp in place, a second to hold the pads in place, and a third to turn the screw without dislodging everything. Since C-clamps are heavy, they really hurt when you drop them on your foot because your third hand took the day off. Plus, it takes time to prep the clamps by backing them off to just the right amount — not too little and not too much or time will be wasted during the critical wet-assembly process. Plus, the oil you put on the threads to keep them working smoothly gets on your hands, which then gets on the pretty wood. Plus, you pay a lot for all this aggravation because C-clamps are not cheap.

The clamps that I now use in many assembly and laminating situations don't cost me a thing. They are the same kind of clamps generations of woodworkers before me have used — way before C-clamps were even invented. They are called wedges and they do everything right that C-clamps do wrong. The broad surface of the wedge eliminates marring and distributes the pressure over a large area without the need for additional pads. The clamping body or frame, also made out of wood, sets up quickly and can help support and align the parts to be joined. You don't need a third hand; in fact, you don't need any hands at all to set the wedge. All it takes is a quick tap or two with a mallet. If that wedge pops out during the unclamping process and lands on your foot, you'll really be glad you weren't using C-clamps.

BLOCKS SCREWED TO TABLE

WEDGES FORCE LAMINATIONS AGAINST FORM

FORM ATTACHED TO PLYWOOD "TABLE"

WAX PAPER PREVENTS GLUING THE LAMINATION TO TABLE

WEDGING LAMINATIONS

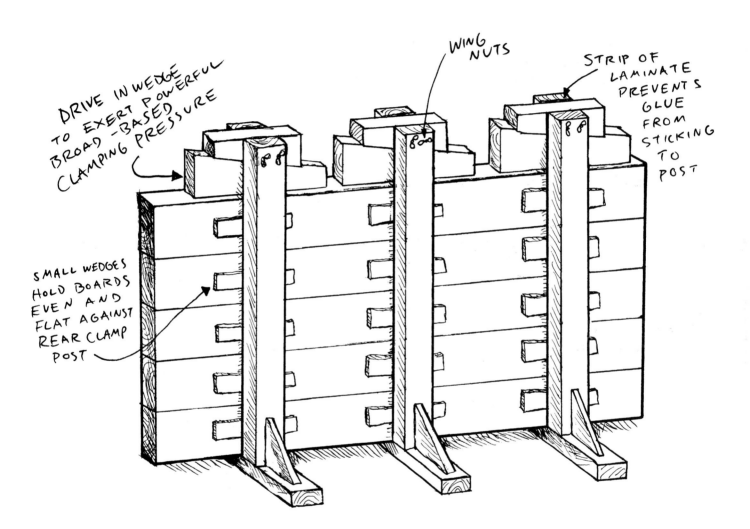

WING NUTS

STRIP OF LAMINATE PREVENTS GLUE FROM STICKING TO POST

DRIVE IN WEDGE TO EXERT POWERFUL BROAD-BASED CLAMPING PRESSURE

SMALL WEDGES HOLD BOARDS EVEN AND FLAT AGAINST REAR CLAMP POST

WEDGE-TYPE COUNTER CLAMP

You will never, ever completely know what you are doing.

At the end of my first day on the job as a boatbuilder-in-training at Penobscot Boat Works on the coast of Maine in the early 1970s, one of the journeymen boatbuilders handed me some C-clamps to put away. He instructed me to open them all the way up, squirt a little oil on the threads, close them back up and then hang them on their storage pegs. Little did I know I was being tested, though I should have guessed by the way he hung around waiting to see how I would go about opening up over a dozen C-clamps. In case you're wondering, I failed the test — handily.

After watching me pick up each clamp in one hand and painstakingly back off the screw with the other, he took pity on me. Without saying so much as a word, he picked up a C-clamp in each hand, gripping them by their T-handle. With his arms hanging down by his side, he made small circular motions that got the body of each clamp moving in a clockwise direction, which automatically opened the clamps. In seconds, two clamps were ready for oiling. He gave me a nod and walked away.

"Good lord," I thought to myself,

"do I have a lot to learn!" Not only are there endless things to learn about using all these tools, there are even things to learn about putting them away. No wonder Bud McIntosh cautioned us not to call ourselves master boatbuilders, or master anything, until we had at least 12 years of intensive, full-time experience under our belts. And now, more than 30 years later, I still think the same way about my vocation — and now avocation — of working at woodworking. There is always something new to learn, some old skill to refine, some clever trick to discover that will make the work go better.

Which is fine with me. If I completely knew what I was doing, I would be bored to death.

my top twenty books

This is a list of the books that have had a profound influence on my life in woodworking. Each one has inspired and informed me in ways that made me a more skilled and successful artisan. This is by no means a complete list of books on the subject of working wood, and I don't mean to imply that these books are required reading for everyone, but I'm sure glad that I read them. I've listed the books in roughly the order in which I read them.

1, 2 & 3
A Museum of Early American Tools
by Eric Sloane
(W. FUNK, 1964)

Back in the late 1960s when I was looking for something, anything, besides a career in corporate America, I happened on this book. Far more than a stuffy book filled with pictures of old tools, this modest black-and-white book was brought to life by Sloane's drawings. While most books on antique tools did little more than give them names, Sloane showed the tools being used! Best of all, his dynamic illustrations made working with these relics from the past look easy and exciting (though when I tried my hand at these tools, the excitement was in much greater abundance than the ease). In any case, I was enthralled. In truth, this is the book that ignited my first spark of interest in woodworking as a craft — a craft that I could picture myself doing. I also recommend Sloane's *Diary of an Early American Boy: Noah Blake, 1850* (W. Funk, 1962) and *A Reverence for Wood* (W. Funk, 1965) for further indulgence in the romance of working wood with preindustrial tools.

4
Foxfire (series)
edited by Eliot Wigginton
(ANCHOR BOOKS, 1972 ET AL.)

Like the Sloane books, the *Foxfire* books show the working life of preindustrial society — what the authors call the "affairs of plain living." These books are a window into the remnants of that society in the Appalachian Mountains. Sloane got me started and the *Foxfire* books kept me going by showing me the tools in the hands of living craftspeople who were still engaged in building fascinating, challenging things. As I was living Thoreau-like in the woods of southern New Hampshire at this time, the *Foxfire* books struck close to home. Here was something I could do living in the woods — and who knows, maybe I'd figure out how to make a living at it.

5
The Complete Woodworker
edited by Bernard E. Jones
(TEN SPEED PRESS, 1980)

For some odd reason Ten Speed Press never tells us that this book is a reprint of an early 20th-century woodworking textbook. Maybe they figured (this was, after all, back in 1980 before woodworking gained its current level of popularity) that no one would notice the difference. But it was just this difference that made the book so appealing to me. Most contemporary woodworking texts focused on using power tools and not much else. *The Complete Woodworker*, written well before tools had cords on them, was all about handwork. I saw things in this book that I had never seen before: how to properly hold a wooden plane, how to position a ripsaw versus a crosscut saw for effective cutting, and what a shooting board looked like. I was also happy to find a large number of layout tricks that I had never seen before in any book or magazine — tricks that I now use on a daily basis in my shop.

6
Hand Tools: Their Ways and Workings
by Aldren A. Watson
(NORTON, 1982)

In my opinion, this is the best book ever written on hand tools. No pretty photos, but absolutely awesome drawings of not just the hand tools, but how your hands should be holding them. That is what you really need to know in order to use them the way they were designed to be used. This book gave me a huge head start in figuring out how to use some of the more esoteric planes (such as the Stanley tongue-and-groove plane). Watson even shows us how to hold the most prosaic of tools — a pair of pliers — so you can easily open and close them as if they were on springs. That trick in itself was worth the price of the book to me. If I could own only one book on hand tools, this would be the one.

7

Restoring, Tuning & Using Classic Woodworking Tools
by Michael Dunbar
(STERLING PUBLISHING CO., 1989)

Well, of course there is no way I would own only one book on hand tools. I had to own this one by Michael Dunbar too. When I first met Michael in the early 1970s he was already making a living working wood with his hands building Windsor chairs at Strawbery Banke in Portsmouth, New Hampshire. What impressed me the most as I watched Michael work was his deftness with the tools. I couldn't believe how quickly he could hollow out a chair seat with what most people would call primitive tools. He made it look almost effortless, and he made it look like fun because he was so obviously having fun. Luckily for us, he decided to write down what he knew about working with hand tools — from restoring them to using them to their fullest potential. This book added much understanding to my already considerable respect for the hand tools of the woodworking trade.

8

How to Build a Wooden Boat
by David C. "Bud" McIntosh
(WOODENBOAT PUBLICATIONS, 1987)

The day I first met the late New England boatbuilder Bud McIntosh he was down in the hold of a schooner's hull setting keel bolts — and singing Homer's *Iliad* in ancient Greek. He stopped when he saw me peeking through a gap in the planks (probably amused by my mouth hanging open in wonder and awe) and asked, "You like boats?" Well, I did, and I was there to ask him a question about planking a skiff I was building for my family.

Bud not only answered that question, but he answered many more boat and woodworking questions over the ensuing years. When I began to combine writing with my woodworking, Bud gave me the most valuable and fundamental piece of advice I needed to hear: "Write what you know, and if you enjoy doing what you know, people will enjoy reading what you have to say about it."

He should know, because that is exactly what he did in his own book. Not only does *How to Build a Wooden Boat* offer us one of the clearest explanations of building a traditional wooden boat ever presented, it does so in a way filled with humor and lively anecdotes. (Don't miss the one about what happened when a bunch of tipsy boatbuilders volunteered to build their late buddy's coffin.) Though I never went on to build boats of this scale myself, I continue to consult Bud's book whenever I want a definitive answer on how to lay out curved components, or design joints to shed water or find an answer to any number of questions where the technology of traditional wooden boats can give us proven answers.

9 & 10

The Furniture Doctor
by George Grotz
(DOUBLEDAY, 1962)
and Adventures in Wood Finishing
by George Frank
(TAUNTON PRESS, 1981)

Early in my woodworking career I toyed with the notion of specializing in furniture restoration. It sounded like a lot more fun than running trim for a living, and I heard tell that it paid a lot better too. Heck, what with the white gloves and all, it was not far from white-collar work. A friend who refinished antiques on the side told me about these two books and I devoured them. Both turned out to be great reads full of invaluable trade secrets, fascinating woodworking history and enticing anecdotes that make you want to go to a party with these guys. Though I soon realized that furniture restoration work was more chemistry than woodworking — and thus not for me — I still find both these books useful for answering questions about finishes and making repairs.

11

How to Build Shaker Furniture
by Thos. Moser
(DRAKE PUBLISHERS, 1977)

These days countless books are available on Shaker furniture. But back in 1977 when I first read this book, there weren't so many. Those that were available generally offered little more than grainy black-and-white photos of historical pieces with little information about their construction. Even so, through these books and visits to several museums I had fallen in love with Shaker furniture. Moser's book was a breakthrough — at least, for me and my circle of friends. His book was filled with clear illustrations that made the joinery look doable, with measured drawings that include some of my most favorite examples of Shaker furniture. This was the first book I owned that inspired me to build a piece right off its pages.

12

The Wheelwright's Shop
by George Sturt
(CAMBRIDGE UNIVERSITY PRESS, 1943)

This quirky paperback is my all-time favorite, number one book on woodworking. It is a book that perhaps makes one exception to the statement I made in the introduction above: this book is required reading. Your reward: you will become fully immersed in a time (the early 1900s) and a place (a wagon-building shop in England) where you will get to know a group of men working and living a life in a preindustrial craft that was unchanged for centuries (but which is nearly extinct today in the western world). George Sturt, the last son of the last owner of a century-old cart and wheelwright shop, reports in great detail not only how these men worked and the tools they worked with, but even more importantly, how they thought.

It's hard for us to really understand how immersed preindustrial craftsmen were in their tools, materials and bodies. Here were people who could shape the complex curves of the draw shaft so it would perfectly match the shape of the horse and the configuration of the front axle of a wagon, without reference to a plan or pattern. The intensity of their training and daily work life made their movements become effortlessly intuitive and appropriate. The only hard part of reading this book is that you know how it's going to end; Sturt's shop and its workers would cease to exist in our own lifetime. It is hard to accept the fact that these men were going to die off along with the centuries-old knowledge and skills that had been passed on to them and honed over the course of their lives.

What's even scarier is the realization that we are the last generation to have known these people, which means that if any of this is not to be lost, then we are the ones who are supposed to carry it on. This makes me, for one, feel very humble and a bit guilty for not having paid more attention to the few craftsmen of that generation I was honored to know. Thanks to Sturt, at least some record of that particular time and place will prevail.

13

Understanding Wood: A Craftsman's Guide to Wood Technology
by R. Bruce Hoadley
(TAUNTON PRESS, 1980)

If there was ever a book to give meaning to the idiom "everything you ever wanted to know about (fill in the blank) but were afraid to ask," *Understanding Wood* is it. Not only does Hoadley give answers to scary questions like "Why did the wood do that?" but he also offers a plethora of answers to questions you probably don't even know you have — but should have if you really want to master this medium. This is where I learned why and how wood moves the way it does and the fundamentals of how to deal with it; why wood shows certain kinds of grain patterns and how they might affect its properties; and how the various properties of wood determine its best usage in structures. This book, in combination with his second book, *Identifying Wood: Accurate Results with Simple Tools*, (Tauton Press, 1990) is all the reference almost any woodworker would need to know and understand wood.

14

Make a Chair from a Tree: An Introduction to Working Green Wood
by John D. Alexander, Jr.
(TAUNTON PRESS, 1978)

In the mid-1970s I lived for a year on a farm on the edge of Appalachia. Under the tutelage of Windsor chairmaker David Sawyer we learned to work green white oak into old-timey farm implements. It was fascinating watching David turn a wrist-size wedge of sopping wet oak into a hayfork in just a couple of hours using just a froe, a drawknife and a saw. After about a week of intense effort, we were doing it too — though

not nearly so fast.

Unfortunately, there was not such a great market for hayforks — even along the Maryland and Pennsylvania border where we lived. There was, however, a market for chairs. Well, David makes exceptionally beautiful chairs using much the same methods and tools, but he had gone off in his Model T back home to Vermont. Fortunately, John Alexander put down on paper what David would have shown us, and he does a pretty good job of it. If you want to try your hand at "busting a chair out of a tree," carefully read this book, gather the right tools and practice what you've read . . . a lot.

15

Welsh Stick Chairs
by John Brown
(LINDEN PUBLISHING CO., 1993)

Well, I never did get into making chairs for a living, but I sure enjoyed reading this book about someone who did: John Brown of Wales. It's a how-to if you are interested in how the Welsh made their traditional, Windsor-like stick chairs, but it's also the story of a man who found his way through working wood with his hands to "live in a beautiful place, work at something I love and make enough money to live." In this cyber-oriented age, I find this heartening to read about.

16

Tage Frid Teaches Woodworking
by Tage Frid
THREE VOLUMES:
Joinery; Shaping, Veneering and Finishing; and Furniture Making
(TAUNTON PRESS, 1979)

In my opinion, if you can't get the opportunity to work with a master furniture maker at some point in your career, then do the next best thing: read this set of books by Tage Frid. Tage was a master teacher as well as woodworker, an attribute that shines through in the concise, step-by-step approach used throughout the books. You have to pay attention, and the photos and drawings aren't the best, but you will learn a lot of essential woodworking processes simply by reading these pages (followed, of course, by putting what you read to the test with real tools and real wood).

17
Fine Woodworking Design Book (series)
from the editors of *Fine Woodworking* magazine
(TAUNTON PRESS, 1977 ET AL.)

When I'm confronted with a furniture design challenge, my process works like this: I begin by looking at historical reference books to see what former generations of furniture makers did to meet the same program (architect-speak for what functions the piece is supposed to fulfill). I try to look past the period styling to discover their unique functional solutions. (This is, admittedly, really difficult for certain periods.) Next, I look to see what my contemporaries are doing to meet this particular program. This design series is where I look first. Here I can see up-to-date, multiple solutions to this same design opportunity in high-quality photographs. It's a hotbed of ideas.

18
Fine Woodworking (magazine)
(TAUNTON PRESS, 1975-93)

In the early 1970s, when my colleagues and I were getting into building fine furniture and custom cabinets, there were essentially no trade magazines for us to read. While plenty of how-to magazines for weekend handymen were available, they didn't offer the advanced techniques or sophisticated designs that we needed to create the kind of furniture we saw coming out of the shops of West Coast masters like Sam Maloof and Art Carpenter or the East Coast art school woodworking shops under teachers like Wendell Castle, Dan Valenza and Tage Frid. Then *Fine Woodworking* showed up. I don't think an issue went by without something I learned from it showing up in my work. In my opinion, a full set of *Fine Woodworking* magazines encompasses the known universe of furniture making and fine cabinetmaking. I refer to my set regularly and get guidance — if not direct answers — to nearly 100 percent of my questions. If you can find a set (the magazine ceased publication in 1993), and you have the shelf space, grab it!

19
Encyclopedia of Furniture Making
by Ernest Joyce
(STERLING PUBLISHING CO., 1987)

If you don't have the shelf space (or money!) for a full collection of back issues of *Fine Woodworking* magazine, then Joyce's book is a good backup until you do. I used this book for years to learn the whys and how-tos of certain joints, how to make tambour doors and how to do basic workshop geometry (to mention just a few examples). Its presentation is rather outdated and some of the terms are British, but in general the information is still sound — especially in the later editions that have been revised by Alan Peters and Patrick Spielman. This book still lives, in fact, on the lower shelf of my in-shop library.

20
The Unknown Craftsman: A Japanese Insight into Beauty
by Sóetsu Yanagi
(KODANSHA INTERNATIONAL, 1972)

Soon after getting into custom furniture and cabinetmaking as a profession, I came to that point where I began to tie my sense of self-worth to what other people thought of my work. Even worse, I began to feel that I was in competition with my fellow woodworkers. Not only did I want their approval, but I thought I must strive to be better than them or I wouldn't achieve distinction (and therefore success). Then, via my explorations into Buddhism, I came across this book. It presented me with a heaping, much needed serving of humble pie by telling me things like, "A beautiful work of art . . . is the work of a man who is not [bound to] either beauty and ugliness or even to himself."

Yanagi was talking about the craftsmen of Japan's past who, working with "total disengagement," created some of the most beautiful art objects the world has ever seen. This work was never signed because these were the products of craftsmen who "made no effort to express their individuality through the medium of things; [instead] they produced things through the medium of man." As my understanding of Buddhism deepened, so did the import of these words. The bottom line was that I relaxed, I let myself enjoy the process and I let the objects I made speak for themselves. Humble pie never tasted so good.

my top twenty tools

When I've been asked to list what I consider the most important, must-have tools of the woodworking trade, people are surprised when I don't immediately rattle off a list of cabinetmaker-grade stationary machines and high-tech hand power tools. Sure, I think all these tools are important, desirable and wonderful, and I know that I, for one, couldn't have made a living without them. Plus, I love all this stuff just as much as any other full-blooded woodworker. But other tools — sometimes the most simple and primitive — have also rewarded me with dramatic increases in production efficiency, raised the level of safety in the shop or contributed significantly to my enjoyment of woodworking. Some of the tools on my list have, in fact, given me all three blessings at the same time. Sources for the specialty tools mentioned here are listed on page 111.

1
A set of decent workbenches

It's hard for me to admit this publicly, but I worked for two out of my three decades of professional woodworking without owning a decent workbench. And *worked* is the operative term here. Without a bench that was solid, that was sized to my height and to the work I did, or that offered decent vises and other holding accessories placed in the right spots, I was making more work for myself. Work that I wasn't getting paid for. Work that I wasn't enjoying.

I finally realized after too many make-do work surfaces that the right workbench with the right accessories does much of the work for you. A properly designed and well-made bench quickly holds stock securely at the right height and working position for all manner of hand and hand-power tooling. An assembly bench or table provides a solid and level surface at a convenient height for putting together components. The assembly table can also double as a stock support for materials that will be fed into the table saw, giving you a much welcomed helping hand.

Other workbenches can be designed to meet specific tasks, such as sharpen-ing or sanding. Storage options hold all the appropriate tools for the task at hand, and specialized accessories, like an integral dust-collection system for the sanding table, make the work safer, more efficient and more pleasant. These specialized workbenches are the keystone of an efficient workstation.

Having enjoyed the fruits of a shop filled with excellent workbenches, I can't imagine what I was thinking in those first two decades. I must have been too busy trying to do work on stock that wasn't properly oriented, or was loose or had fallen on the floor.

2
A horse, in team with a drawknife and a spokeshave

Of all the hand tools I've introduced my hands to, the drawknife is the one that has proven to be absolutely the most versatile and most fun to use. Simply no other tool can do what it does, which is to quickly and accurately (with practice) remove slices from a length of wood in nearly complete, dust-free silence. It doesn't do so indiscriminately either. Instead, following the will of my hands, the drawknife almost effortlessly follows the grain of the wood as close as I want it to. This is crucial if I'm making ladder rungs or tool handles, where I must avoid grain run-out (and thus potential shear failure under heavy loads). This same maneuverability also allows me to make the tool follow complex curves, inside and out. But it can play rough too, quickly knocking off corners of boards and removing deep millmarks and defects prior to finish smoothing with other tools.

If I want to smooth the scalloped surfaces characteristically left behind by the drawknife and/or to smooth areas of rough grain, I'll switch to a spokeshave. I don't use the metal-type shaves; I never got used to them, finding them hard to control. Instead, I use the wood-bodied type that holds the blade in the base so that the flat of the blade contributes to the shoe of the tool. This makes the tool highly controllable and less likely to chatter and mar the surface of the wood. The surface left behind by a sharp spokeshave needs no sanding.

So where does the horse come in? Well that's what the traditional name for the shop-made, foot-operated clamp that supports and holds lengths of wood in appropriate positions for the drawknife and spokeshave. An ancient tool, the shaving horse involves you in a symbiotic relationship during the shaving process. As you pull against the wood with the drawknife, your feet automatically brace against the foot board that produces the clamping action. The harder you pull the knife, the harder you push the board and thus the harder the horse grabs onto the board for you. Yet when you release the pressure, the board is instantly free so you can turn it for shaving another facet. Best of all, through the whole process you are sitting comfortably (and you can really get carried away carving the seat to perfectly fit your behind). I've spent many an entire day on the horse (when I was making chairs and farm implements from green wood when I lived in Pennsylvania) and enjoyed myself immensely. I have yet to find another facet of woodworking where you get to sit at a comfortable seat all day, producing finished components while making hardly a sound and nary a speck of sawdust.

3
Swivel-handled scraper

Scrapers in general must be among my top 20 as there is simply no better way to smooth hardwoods with difficult grain structure. When you can't plane it smooth, you can always scrape it smooth. The trick is to learn how to get a really sharp, yet strong burr on the scraper's edge. The secret is to get the blade really sharp first. I hone the blade (while mounted in a fixture to maintain the angle) on a progression of waterstones or microfinishing paper fixed to a flat plate. Most mounted scrapers are ground at 45°, while the thin, handheld types are square. Even that 90° corner, however, should be razor-sharp for best results. The next crucial key is to be sure that your burnisher is free of nicks and other roughness. That roughness will transfer to the burr. Because the

burnisher must be harder than the steel of the blade, I get best results from a real burnishing tool, though I get OK results with the back of some of my gouges and even one of my old cabinet-maker's screwdrivers (which has a highly hardened shank). The final key is to press that burnisher really hard against the blade edge to draw a smooth, solid burr. If you're pressing hard, you need to make only two to three strokes to get a good working burr.

I like using handled scraper blades for this important reason: the blades get incredibly hot. You can actually burn your fingers on a scraper blade in hard action. (Plane blades get hot too, but you never feel them because they are buried in the body of the plane.) It's also hard to hold the blade at the most effective cutting angle during a sweeping motion. After using a handled scraper for a year, I stumbled across an old scraper tool that featured a ball-and-socket joint where the handle joined the blade holder. With a little twist, I can loosen the handle and adjust it to any angle I want. This puts my hands at a much better angle for pulling, as I'm usually standing to the side of the board at the bench. A small bar behind the blade holder provides a grip for my second hand and puts force right behind the blade where it's needed most. This tool makes scraping — generally a highly aerobic task — much easier, more fun and more effective.

4
Waterstone sharpening system and microfinishing paper blade-flattening system

One of my mentors once told me that the best thing to do with my oilstones was to chuck them out the window of the boat shop where we working. That

way, they would sink to the bottom of Rockport Harbor and I would never have to deal with them again. I looked at my trusty old oilstones that night and saw what he meant: lurking under a grimy rag, they were dished from use because I never seemed to get around to flattening them on the belt sander. That's because when I did they clogged the paper with oily grit. Of course, the poorly maintained stones meant my plane and chisel blades were getting dished too, having been forced to take the shape of the stone. Then there was the usual mess of oil on my hands as I handled them — oil that would too often find its way onto the wood I was working with if I didn't take the time to thoroughly wash my hands. As if that was going to happen with any regularity!

The next day I went to town and bought a set of Japanese waterstones, and after one more day I took my mentor's advice and chucked the oilstones in the salt chuck. I never once regretted doing that. The waterstones sharpen my cutters at probably twice the speed of my old oilstones, and they are always absolutely flat because it takes just a moment to keep them that way. (I flatten the coarsest stone on a diamond plate, then flatten the other stones to the coarse one with just a few strokes.) Because there is no oil involved, my hands are much easier to wash clean.

In the last several years I installed a Tormek water grinding stone system in my shop. Though it doesn't produce a sharper edge than the flat stones, it does produce the razor-sharp edges in half the time. Because the stone turns slowly and is constantly cooled by water, it can never change or destroy the temper of my cutters — something a regular grinding wheel can do all too easily. My system has a wide selection of available fixtures to hold, at a precise angle to the wheel, blades of all kinds from chisels, to plane irons, to axe heads, to scissors, to esoteric carving tools, to 12" planer blades. In general, I sharpen the bevel of my plane irons and chisels on the wheel, and then hone the back of the blades on my flattened waterstones.

That is, if the backs of my blades are already essentially flat. If not, I use a microfinishing paper sharpening system made by Mark Duginske to get and to keep them that way. It's a simple process: you set the fixture in a vise, install a sheet of paper on the flat plate-glass table with the screw hold-downs and then rub the back of the blade on the paper, using water for a lubricant. For initial flattening, I start with the coarsest paper, working my way up to the finest until I get a perfectly flat, mirrorlike finish.

Precision fence and stop gauge systems on stationary tools

The day I installed a decent fence and gauge system on two machines — my 10" cabinet saw and chop saw — was the day I started to actually make a profit at woodworking. That's because from that day on I stopped using one of the most time-wasting, error-prone tools that ever found a place in my shop: the tape measure. Because these accessories allowed me to set the machines to their own rules in seconds with no margin of error between them, I never needed to set a fence or stop to my tape measure again. Simply put, if I wanted a panel to be ripped 18" wide according to my cutting list, that's where I put the cursor on the rip fence. If I wanted to cut a board 8" long to match the panel, I set the cursor of the chop saw to that number and chopped away. As long as I checked the cursors by cutting scraps at the begin-

ning of the process, I enjoyed a fail-safe system for cutting stock to cutting lists with incredible precision and speed.

Saddle square

Even though I rarely do hand joinery in my production work, I still enjoy being productive. So when Bridge City Tool Works sent me a saddle square to try out, I paid attention because the layout of the cut lines is probably the most difficult and time-consuming portion of creating a simple joint. What the saddle square does is allow you to lay out two sides of the joint at the same time. Not only does this save time by cutting in half the number of times you must square to a mark, but the design of the tool assures that the lines will match perfectly and be absolutely square to the corner it's held to. Plus, it's a beautiful tool to look at. Another version of the saddle square features a blade with angled sides (one at 8:1 and the other at 6:1) hinged to a straight-sided blade. You will use this tool, as I'm sure you have already guessed, to mark dovetails.

High-end, low-angle block plane

The very first hand tool I bought for myself was an old Stanley low-angle block plane. Because part of the casting was chipped, the junk store guy in Barrington, New Hampshire, let me have it for 50 cents. I used that plane on an almost daily basis for nearly 20 years, and I still have it today (though it now enjoys a well-deserved retirement). The little plane got an early retirement because it got replaced by an upstart made in Maine by Thomas Lie-Nielsen.

The Lie-Nielsen low-angle, manganese-bodied plane earned its place in my apron not only because it's so pretty,

but because it works so much better than the old Stanley ever did. Not that there was anything wrong with the Stanley; even though it was chipped, it worked as well as it was designed to. The secret to Lie-Nielsen's plane, however, is a better design. While the Stanley relies on an unrefined casting to support the blade, the Lie-Nielsen features milled surfaces that provide a broad surface for the blade to securely rest upon at a precise angle. Also, the blade of the Lie-Nielsen is much thicker than the Stanley, a feature that resists chattering. The slightly harder steel also helps the Lie-Nielsen stay sharper longer. Finally, the hold-down cap of the Lie-Nielsen, smooth as a worry stone, fits my palm perfectly. It just feels good to have it in my hand. These days, the Stanley feels best as a fond memory.

Plunge router

I've been in woodworking long enough to remember when routers were little more than a motor with a handle stuck on the side. To me, they were basically a powered moulding plane. When the plunge mechanism was finally made widely available, it was really a reinvention of the tool. Suddenly, the router could do so many more things with safety and precision. The possibilities for the humble router were magnified enormously. Instead of using routers just for shaping edges and hogging away material, I now began using them for everything from making mortises to creating complex recesses for fine inlay work. Once routers could take the plunge, they joined the ranks of my indispensable hand tools.

9

Japanese-style saws

Not much chance you will have read it here first, but Japanese-type saws work much better than western-style saws in most applications. It takes a while for us cowboys to get used to a saw that cuts on the pull rather than the push stroke, but it's worth getting used to. Because the blades are under a tension load only during the cutting phase, they can be much thinner than push blades. That means the kerf is smaller, which means the amount of material you have to cut away with your muscles is smaller. And that's a good thing when you are working wood by hand. The blades are also generally a harder steel than western blades, which helps them stay sharp longer. The coarsest cutting saw that I own is a Japanese timber saw with a 2'-long blade. The finest saw that I own is a Japanese dovetail saw that features a slightly curved blade and teeth as fine as the hair on a gnat's back.

The one application where I do not use a Japanese-type saw (unless it's one of the hybrids with Japanese-style teeth and a thick western-style blade) is when I'm hand-ripping boards. I like the blade to cut on the push stroke because that allows me to put my weight behind it, and I just can't get used to pulling a saw from underneath a board with the same amount of force and speed.

10

Foam brushes

I'll admit it, one of the primary reasons I now use foam brushes for applying everything from glue to spar varnish is because I'm lazy. I really don't enjoy cleaning brushes, which often takes as long as the time it took to use the brush in the first place. I really like the fact that when I'm done applying the finish or glue, I can just chuck the brush in

the waste bin. It costs me something, but not that much since I buy them by the box. (I buy 2½" width, which works for the majority of tasks. If I need a narrower brush, I cut it down with scissors.) Over time I probably spend more replacing an expensive bristle brush after one too many times of not having washed it thoroughly than the dozen or so foam brushes used for the same amount of work.

Even if I wasn't lazy, however, I still would have switched over. That's because not only are foam brushes cheap, but they seem to work as well as — and sometimes better than — most bristle brushes. I did a comparison test, pitting my best natural-bristle brush against a foamie. Spreading paint, the foamie produced fewer brushstrokes than did the bristle. When used for spreading varnish, the foam did make more bubbles than the bristle, though because the varnish was warm and low in viscosity, the bubbles did break before the tack set in. One drawback with the foam was that it did not hold quite as much fluid, which meant I had to dip a bit more often. Another drawback was that after about 10 minutes the foam lost some stiffness and started to fold over during the brushstrokes. Of course, that was easily fixed by chucking it and replacing it with a new one. This does rouse some feelings of having become a throwaway consumer . . . tempered by not stinking up the environment with brush cleaners all the time!

11

Wax (spray or candle)

I could hardly believe it, but after ripping only six boards the table saw was starting to feel really dull to me. Each successive board was harder to push through than the last, yet I had just put a sharp blade on the arbor. Then I had a

vision: my old woodshop teacher pulling a funky old candle out of his pocket, his "jiffy sharpening stick." Sure enough, a quick cleanup of the saw table with a squirt of kerosene followed by a few swipes of candle wax and the feed was back up to speed — just as if I had put a new blade on the saw. In fact, the blade wasn't getting dull; my attention was. I should have thought about the fact that the pitch commonly found in pine boards is incredibly sticky stuff and that when it gets on the table surfaces it quickly bogs down the feed.

My use of the "jiffy sharpening stick" isn't limited to machine tables. I use it regularly on the base of hand planes, power planes, hand and power saws and even on the threads of screws. The wax not only reduces friction (which reduces the effort required from you as the feeder), but also slows down the buildup of pitch and other residues. That's why, like my old shop teacher, I keep a stub of candle as an essential component of my shop aprons and tool belts.

12

Any and all cordless handheld power tools

It's sometimes hard for me to believe, but I've been in the construction trade long enough to remember the days before cordless power tools. I do remember clearly, however, days filled with hatred for cords. My most cogent memories usually involve scaffolding. Oh, how I loved it when the last hole to be drilled or the last line of the cut was just beyond the reach of the power cord. So it was back down the scaffold to the truck for another piece of extension cord, which wasn't there, so it was back up the scaffolding to untie the cord so I could reroute it to another outlet, which wasn't there because this was a new construction site with a single "temp" pole. Other fond memories include visions of tripping over cords that shouldn't be where they were (again up on the scaffolding in one particularly vivid memory) and watching drill cords — pulled by some unseen force in another room — get caught under a table saw, nearly tipping it over onto a freshly laid hardwood floor. So when they finally got battery technology up to the point where a drill would actually drive a bunch of screws and a trim saw would actually cut off a piece of trim more than once, I was first in line to buy. I now own six cordless drills, a cordless jig saw, a cordless trim saw and I'm looking at the new cordless router just out on the market.

13
Double-sided tape

I often need to hold some parts together temporarily; gang cutting identical components or holding a cutting pattern in place during milling are two typical examples in my shop. I used to think the only safe and secure way to do this was to either fasten them together with screws (which meant being sure the holes wouldn't show) or, if screw holes would show no matter where I put them, to glue the parts together with kraft paper in between. But screws are time-consuming to install, and glue (even with the paper buffer) is a pain to remove. Then one day I watched carpet installers use a strip of heavy-duty carpet tape to hold down a piece of carpet in a hard-to-reach area. Eureka! If tape can hold down heavy carpet in the hallway of First Federal, I thought to myself, I could certainly use it to hold a piece of $1/4$" pattern stock to a workpiece. As I drove home, more applications popped into my mind: holding a spiling board in place on a rough-cut plank, holding drawer faces temporarily in position

against their boxes for locating fastenings, pasting cutoffs of curved legs back in place so they will support the leg for cutting the side curve, and so on.

Using carpet tape as a temporary fastener is not only fast, but it's secure for all my typical applications. It's so strong, in fact, that I have to be careful when wedging stuff apart not to mar the work. I use a small crowbar or a chisel as a wedge, if possible working the parting tool in areas of the workpiece that won't be seen after installation. But unlike the kraft paper trick, once the parts let go, the tape rolls right off, rarely leaving any residue to clean up. I can't imagine ever going back to screws or glue since that day when I laughed all the way home from the bank.

14
Stick-on sandpaper

Speaking of sticky tape, I'd like to shake the hand of the guy who thought up making sticky-backed sandpaper and selling it by the roll. Ever since I discovered that you could buy rolls of high-quality sandpaper with an adhesive backing, I have not bought a single sheet of sandpaper. With the sandpaper mounted like a roll of toilet paper (I make up a board with an old hacksaw blade for a cutter), I can pull out any length I need, depending on where I'm sticking it. I instantly apply the paper to the base of my power sanders, block sanders and chunks of wood or foam shaped to a particular curve. Sometimes I pull out a random short length and simply fold it over on itself to hand-sand a small area. At this point, I can't even think of an application where I would need a typical sheet of sandpaper. And if I did, I would probably hate the fact that there wasn't stickum on the back of it!

15
Aftermarket see-through router base

You would have thought that the people who make routers would have thought it nice to install a clear base that you could see through so you could see the stop marks, or the end of the board, or the cord that sometimes gets itself in the way. They didn't, but thankfully inventor/woodworker Pat Warner did. Pat makes a line of clear, acrylic bases that are presized and machined to fit on a wide variety of common routers. The one I own features an offset that not only provides a knob for getting a better grip, but adds welcome additional surface area when I'm working near the ends or outside corners of a workpiece. Needless to say, this is the router (and I have eight of them!) that I most often grab for doing freehand routing.

16
Biscuit joiners

Ah yes, the great biscuit joiner controversy: Do spline biscuits really constitute a woodworking joint? Well, I don't know the answer to that, but I do know that ever since I started using biscuits to join face frames and other common casework components I started seeing a real jump in my bottom line. I don't trust biscuits for situations where there will be a lot of load on the joint, but where the structures are fully supported (as face frames are) I have no qualms about using them. I've rarely seen a biscuit-joined connection fail, and when I did, it was due to operator error (which was me: I didn't put enough glue in the slots, which meant there wasn't enough glue to make the biscuits swell and really grab). I have yet to find a faster way to fasten two pieces of wood or panels together with a glued, wood-to-wood joint — which, come to think of it, sounds suspiciously like a woodworking joint.

17
Miniature power feeder

For all but the last five years of my woodworking career, I was the power feeder in my shop. I always thought that electric power feeders were for the big boys. To this small-time operator, they were an extravagance I just couldn't afford. Besides, I figured, I can do what they do just about as well. But I couldn't really. For one thing, I didn't have the energy or strength to feed board after board tight to the shaper or table saw fence and table surface at a consistent rate — which meant stock burned when I went too slowly, or went off the cut line as I tired.

So when power feeders came down in price — and size — I went for one. I installed a miniature feeder on my router table and have hardly used it without the feeder since. It not only does all the work for you, it does it better than you could ever hope to. I can adjust the rate of feed to match the type of cut and wood so that burning or scalloping is never a problem. Set correctly, the feeder pushes the wood slightly against the fence as well as the table surface so that the cuts are straight and consistent. Best of all, at the end of the workday, my muscles aren't screaming at me.

18
Throat plate with replaceable wood insert

Take a close look at your table saw. Most likely, you'll see that the throat plate that came with the saw leaves nearly a $\frac{1}{4}$" gap around the blade. The manufacturer made it this way to allow the plate to be used at any blade tilt angle, but it compromises the saw's ability to make smooth cuts on the underside of the

stock. Even worse, cutting stock narrower than the gap can be downright dangerous. That's because the stock is entirely unsupported next to the blade and can jam against the far end of the throat plate opening, causing a kickback.

To solve this problem, I upgraded my saw with an aftermarket throat plate. The plate features a replaceable wood strip that slides into place on the aluminum plate. I keep a number of strips ready to go, each cut for my most common blade angles (0°, 22$\frac{1}{2}$°, 30° and 45°). I use others for common dado blade settings. And I put in a new blank strip when I'm cutting delicate veneered plywood or very narrow stock. Of course, you can alternatively make your own throat plates out of melamine, using the stock one as a template. The point is: Don't use the stock throat plate for anything but rough cuts where the gap will be wider than the blade-to-throat gap.

19
Pocket hole jigs

Sometimes you don't need to make joints; you just need to screw things together. When you are looking for a fast way to fasten together fully supported face frames, or to install dividers in a drawer, or to draw stock snugly together during a gluing procedure, fastening can prevail over joinery. In these cases I reach for my Kreg pocket hole jig. Because it holds my hand drill at a shallow angle while I make the pilot hole, the point of the screw will come out near the center of a board — perfect for drawing the board to its mating surface. This jig offers me the fastest way I know of to draw two workpieces together while creating a joint that is as strong as the screws that go into the holes.

20
The washable dust mask

Starting out in woodworking, when my enthusiasm was matched only by my naïveté, I never wore dust masks even when immersed in the spewing clouds of an intense sanding spree. When my brain finally caught up with the fact that my allergies were peaking in direct relation to those episodes in the shop, I realized it might be a good idea to reduce the amount of dust that was going into my lungs. So I went out and bought a disposable paper dust mask with a single little strand of rubber to hold it to my face, which at that time included a beard. Being a cheapskate, I used the same mask for days. Not that it really mattered as it hardly worked anyway. No way that little rubber band was going to create a seal around my nose and mouth, especially since it was fighting a beard.

When the sneezing fits persisted over weekends, I decided to upgrade to the professional version of the dust mask, which featured a thicker mask and two heavy-duty rubber straps. I even shaved my beard. It worked better at filtering out the dust, but (as you have probably also experienced) these masks are stuffy, restrictive and thus hard to wear for any length of time. Plus, they cost a lot more than the handyman/homeshop version, which meant I was even more begrudging about chucking them. I shudder to think of all the bacteria that found a home in those masks over the weeks they hung damp on a hook.

My next upgrade was to a helmet featuring a belt-mounted, battery-powered fan that kept a stream of clean air flowing across my face. This was a great improvement in keeping the dust out of my lungs, with the added benefit of providing a shield that protected my eyes during milling operations. But the helmet had its drawbacks too. The helmet and battery pack feel a bit heavy after a while, and the whole rig takes about a minute to put on, which meant I often skipped putting it on when I was going to make only a quick cut or two on the saw. Then I discovered a washable mask at the Wooden Boat Festival here in Port Townsend, Washington, last year.

It was no surprise that it was designed, and now sold, by a working woodworker, a woodturner named Paula Nicks of Fort Myers, Florida. Here was a safety product that pushed all the right buttons: it is easy to put on, the hook and loop straps make it almost instantaneous, the polyester mesh filters dust as well as if not better than the thick paper masks and the microfibers of the mask are breathable — much less restrictive than the paper types. This means I tend to keep the mask on most of the time I'm in the shop, not just when I'm actually producing dust. This also means all those microfine particles that are nearly always floating around in the shop don't get the opportunity to lodge in my lungs. (The medics tell us that it is the finest, floating particles that do the most harm in our bodies anyway.) And best of all for this cheapskate, I never need throw the mask away when it gets dirty because these masks are designed to be washed and reused as many times as you want.

My Top Tools Runners-Up

Flat-faced clamps

These clever holding devices turn any table surface less than 36" wide into a panel or board clamping station. If you don't enjoy the services of the vise and dog system of a traditional workbench, this is a great poor man's substitute. I have used these flat clamps for years.

Quick-release clamps

Another clamp that came into widespread use in the last decade or so is the quick-release throat clamp. Not only do they clamp down with one hand, some versions release with just one hand as well. Another advantage is that the heads are made of a nonmarring plastic. Though these clamps won't bear down as hard as a traditional throat clamp, it's not often you need that magnitude of clamping force. And if you do, there's a good chance you are doing something wrong!

Hole jigs

Building casework, I often need to drill long lines of perfectly aligned holes to accept shelf-support hardware and Euro-style hardware fittings. This jig, which accepts a plunge router instead of a drill (which is more common), makes the hole-making go fast and with great precision.

Water mister

The fastest way to get fine floating dust out of the shop — which is important if you are about to spread on surface finishes like varnish — is to make it fall out of the air. To make fine dust fall, you simply make it heavy, which you can do easily by misting the air with water. I learned this trick from Pat Cudahy, a professional photographer I've had the pleasure to work with over the years.

Ball rollers

A little ball in a cup may not seem all that significant or exciting, but this device has saved — and continues to save — my hide. That's because these low-cost pieces of hardware go wherever I need a helping hand while working alone in the shop. Installed in a gang on top of feed tables or on side fences, they support sheet stock and other large items as I feed the stuff through the saw. What puts ball rollers on the list over typical cylindrical rollers (which typically find their way into commercial supports) is the fact that they are balls. While cylindrical rollers impart a direction to the stock, balls don't. That means they are never fighting you; they are working only to support the weight of the stock. Of course, you can set up the cylinders to feed the stock in the correct direction (usually slightly against the fence), but if they shift for any reason, watch out! I recommend cylinders only on supports that are fixed in relation to the cutting blade, never for free-standing type supports.

HEPA-filtered vacuum with automatic start

Speaking of fine dust, my shop has been a lot freer of the stuff since I replaced my old shop vacuum with a HEPA-filtered vacuum. Its fine-meshed filters catch the tiny dust particles that the Shop Vac misses completely (in fact, it tends to spread them). The autostart feature allows me to plug my sander into the vacuum with both cord and vacuum hose. When I turn on the sander, the vacuum comes on too. I keep my sander in a box all set up with a hose so it's ready in a minute to plug in.

Miniature Japanese-made roundover plane

It may not seem like much, but the one hand tool that has probably spent the most time in my hand is this little wooden hand plane. With its concave cutter, I quickly knock sharp edges off boards and panels — which is often all the edge treatment that I'm looking for. It's cute, it's tiny and it's lightweight enough to ride with me almost unnoticed in a pocket of my overalls. This brings me to another favorite tool.

Carhartt overalls

A tool almost forgotten, not because they aren't important, but because they are so much a part of me I hardly even think about them, is my everyday workshop companion: my Carhartt overalls. I pull them on over my jeans and flannel shirt whenever I walk into the shop to work — and take them off, leaving behind all the dust and grime of the day's work when I go back up into the house. Made of heavy canvas in

Carhartt's signature orange/tan color (which pleases the boatbuilders because their favorite brand of bedding compound blends right in), they feature riveted, doubled fabric not just at the knee but all the way up your lap. This article of clothing will last longer than you want it to; you get tired of carrying around all the layers of paint and glue that accumulate on it over the months and years. Multiple pockets and loops allow me to use the overalls as a work apron in which I carry the following items even as I speak:

- Pen, pencil and eraser
- Ear plugs
- Small (6") combination square
- Spiling block and/or short story sticks (when I'm laying out, taking off or transferring dimensions)
- Bevel gauge and bevel board (when I'm working with angles)
- Dividers
- Tape measure
- a Handkerchief
- One half-eaten Kit Kat bar

suppliers

BRIDGE CITY TOOL WORKS
920 NE 58th Avenue, Suite 100
Portland, Oregon 97213-3786
800-253-3332
www.bridgecitytools.com
Hand planes

CARHARTT, INC.
P.O. Box 600
5750 Mercury Drive
Dearborn, Michigan 48126
www.carhartt.com
Overalls

DUST BEE GONE
Pajo, Inc.
226 Palmacea Road
Fort Myers, Florida 33905
239-694-3627
www.dustbeegone.com
Washable dust masks

FEIN POWER TOOLS
1030 Alcon Street
Pittsburgh, Pennsylvania 15220
800-441-9878
www.feinus.com
Fein vacuums

JAPAN WOODWORKER
1731 Clement Avenue
Alameda, CA 94501
800-537-7820
*Janpanese planes and other
hand tools*

KREG TOOL COMPANY
201 Campus Drive
Huxley, Iowa 50124
800-447-8638
www.kregtool.com
Pocket hole jigs

LEE VALLEY TOOLS LTD.
P.O. Box 1780
Ogdensburg, New York 13669-
6780
800-267-8735
www.leevalley.com
*Fine woodworking tools and
hardware*

LIE-NIELSEN TOOLWORKS
P.O. Box 9
Warren, Maine 04864-0009
800-327-2520
www.lie-nielsen.com
Woodworking hand tools

PAT WARNER
pat@patwarner.com
www.patwarner.com
*Clear sub-bases for routers and
many other innovative router
accessories*

**ROCKLER WOODWORKING AND
HARDWARE**
4365 Willow Drive
Medina, Minnesota 55340
800-279-4441
www.rockler.com
Woodworking tools and hardware

STATES INDUSTRIES
29545 Enid Road, East
P.O. Box 7037
Eugene, Oregon 97401
800-626-1981
www.statesind.com
ApplePly hardwood plywood

TORMEK AB
Box 152
SE-711 23 Lindesberg
Sweden
Phone: +46 581-147 90
webmail@tormek.se
www.tormek.se
Tormek water wheel

VAUGHAN
11414 Maple Avenue
Hebron, Illinois 60034
815-648-2446
www.vaughanmfg.com
Hammers and other tools

WMH TOOL GROUP
2420 Vantage Drive
Elgin, Illinois 60123
847-851-1000
www.wmhtoolgroup.com
Power tools

WOODCRAFT
P.O. Box 1686
Parkersburg, West Virginia
26102-1686
800-225-1153
www.woodcraft.com
*Woodworking hardware and
accessories*

WOODHAVEN
501 West 1st Avenue
Durant, IA 52747-9729
800-344-6657
www.woodhaven.com
Jig and table saw accessories

WOODWORKER'S HARDWARE
P.O. Box 180
Sauk Rapids, Minnesota 56379-
0180
800-383-0130
www.wwhardware.com
*Woodworking tools and acces-
sories; finishing supplies; books
and plans*

WOODWORKING FASTTRACK INC.
W5823 School Avenue
Merrill, WI 54452
715-536-7449
www.woodworkingfasttrack.com
*Sharpening systems, jig acces-
sories and miter gauges*

index